Philosophy of Early Childhood Education

Philosophy of Early Childhood Education

Transforming Narratives

Edited by
Sandy Farquhar and Peter Fitzsimons

Book compilation © 2008 Philosophy of Education Society of Australasia
First published as a special issue of *Educational Philosophy and Theory* (volume 39, issue 3)

BLACKWELL PUBLISHING
350 Main Street, Malden, MA 02148-5020, USA
9600 Garsington Road, Oxford OX4 2DQ, UK
550 Swanston Street, Carlton, Victoria 3053, Australia

First published 2008 by Blackwell Publishing Ltd

1   2008

Library of Congress Cataloging-in-Publication Data

Philosophy of early childhood education: transforming narratives/edited by Sandy Farquhar and Peter Fitzsimons.
    p. cm.
Includes bibliographical references and index.
ISBN 978-1-4051-7404-6 (pbk.: alk. paper) 1. Early childhood education–Philosophy. I. Farquhar, Sandy. II. Fitzsimons, Peter.
    LB1139.23.P49 2007
    371.2101–dc22   2007042068

A catalogue record for this title is available from the British Library.

Set in 10pt Plantin
by Graphicraft Limited, Hong Kong
Printed and bound in Singapore
by C.O.S. Printers Pte Ltd

For further information on
Blackwell Publishing, visit our website at
www.blackwellpublishing.com

Contents

Notes on Contributors   vii

Foreword
MICHAEL A. PETERS   1

Introduction
SANDY FARQUHAR & PETER FITZSIMONS   3

1 **Meetings Across the Paradigmatic Divide**
   PETER MOSS   7

2 **The Gift Paradigm in Early Childhood Education**
   GENEVIEVE VAUGHAN & EILA ESTOLA   24

3 **Conceptions of the Self in Early Childhood:**
   Territorializing identities
   LISELOTT BORGNON   42

4 **Deconstructing and Transgressing the Theory—Practice**
   dichotomy in early childhood education
   HILLEVI LENZ TAGUCHI   52

5 **In Early Childhood: What's language about?**
   LIANE MOZÈRE   68

6 **The Politics of Processes and Products in Education:**
   An early childhood metanarrative crisis?
   ANDREW GIBBONS   76

7 **(Re)Positioning the Child in the Policy/Politics of**
   Early Childhood
   CHRISTINE WOODROW & FRANCES PRESS   88

   Index   102

Notes on Contributors

Sandy Farquhar is an educational designer and senior lecturer in the Faculty of Education at the University of Auckland. She began her teaching in Kindergartens and after a career in publishing is now designing and developing curriculum for teacher education and lecturing in early childhood curriculum studies. Her current research draws on the work of Paul Ricoeur examining the relationship between narrative identity and early childhood.

Peter Fitzsimons has at various times been a teacher, a professional musician, a radio journalist, a factory manager, a harassed parent, and an educational management consultant – including four years managing an early childhood teachers college. With a recent PhD on Nietzsche and Education, his current research interest in ethics focusses on the impact of biotechnology on formulations of the self.

Liselotte Borgnon is a PhD student at the Stockholm Institute of Education in Sweden, where she is a member of the research group for Ethical and Aesthetical Learning processes. Liselotte is currently working on a thesis called *A Virtual Child* where the notion of the identity of the learning pre-school child is being troubled by using experiences from Swedish pre-schools, where transformations regarding the identity of the pre-school child is taking place. Her perspective draws on the work of the French philosophers Gilles Deleuze and Félix Guattari.

Eila Estola is a senior researcher with the Faculty of Education in the Department of Educational Sciences and Teacher Education, University of Oulu, Finland. Her background is in early childhood education. Her main research interests centre on narrative-biographical teacher research, especially on moral dimensions of teaching and teacher identity. She is deeply involved in the project of teacher life (http://www.oulu.fi/ktk/life/english/frontp.htm). Her PhD was about relational morals in teachers' stories. She also has researched the meaningfulness of the body in teaching and the meanings of storytelling in teachers' discussion groups. This article is part of the project 208745 funded by the Academy of Finland.

Andrew Gibbons is a lecturer at the New Zealand Tertiary College. His doctoral thesis, *The Matrix Ate My Baby: Play, technology and the early childhood subject*, problematised contemporary research of the child's play with new technologies. He has a certificate of journalism and a diploma of teaching in early childhood education, and has worked in early education services in Aotearoa/New Zealand and Great Britain. He has published papers examining the philosophy of early education with a focus on play and development, and a particular emphasis on promoting philosophy in the study and practice of early education in Aotearoa/New Zealand. His work at New Zealand Tertiary College includes the development of the publication *He Kupu* exploring issues associated with the delivery of distance education.

Peter Moss is Professor of Early Childhood Provision at the Thomas Coram Research Unit, Institute of Education University of London. His areas of research include services for children, the workforce in these services and the relationship between employment and caring. Much of his work has been cross-national, and he was Coordinator of the European Commission Childcare Network from 1986 to 1996. Recent publications include *From Children's Services to Children's Spaces* (with Pat Petrie), *Care Work: Present and future* (edited with Claire Cameron and Janet Boddy) and *Ethics and Politics in Early Childhood Education* (with Gunilla Dahlberg).

Liane Mozère is a free-lance researcher in a group founded by Félix Guattari in 1965, collaborating with Michel Foucault, benefiting from the intellectual enlightenment of Gilles Deleuze. She was the first Associate Professor at the University of Rouen, and since 2001 has been Professor in Sociology at the University of Metz. Since 2003 she has been a key member of the International group *Reconceptualizing Early Childhood*, engaging in numerous research topics in gender issues. She has written a number of articles (in English) on early childhood; she is writing an introduction for a French translation of Joan Tronto's book *Moral Boundaries*; and she is currently using Deleuze and Guattari's ideas in empirical research on Filipina domestic workers in Paris.

Frances Press is a senior lecturer in early childhood at Charles Sturt University, Bathurst. She has written extensively on early childhood policy in the Australian context, including co-authoring the Australian Background Report to the OECD Thematic Review of Early Childhood Education and Care (with Alan Hayes), and more recently, *What About the Kids? Policy directions for improving the experiences of infants and young children in a changing world*. In collaboration with Christine Woodrow she has been tracing the impact of childcare corporatisation on early childhood policy and understandings of childhood and children's citizenship. In conjunction with her colleague Jennifer Sumsion, she is co-editing two editions of *Contemporary Issues in Early Childhood* that focus on child care policy.

Hillevi Lenz Taguchi is Associate Professor in Education at the Institute of Education in Stockholm, and currently holds a research position as Junior Research Fellow. She received her PhD in Education in 2001, with a dissertation on observational and documentational practices in Early Childhood Education, doing a genealogical study, as well as a feminist poststructural inspired participative ethnography. In addition to teaching and supervision, she is responsible for Reggio Emilia inspired teacher education. Since 2004 she has held the Chair of a Centre of Gender in Educational Sciences at the Institute of Education in Stockholm. Her current research is an externally funded interdisciplinary project on participation, democracy and gender in higher education. The theoretical and methodological framework is feminist poststructural. She has published in Sweden, Europe, and the United States.

Genevieve Vaughan, author of *For-Giving, a Feminist Criticism of Exchange*, is a lecturer, social change activist, and founder of the feminist Austin, Texas-based Foundation for a Compassionate Society 1988–1998. Vaughan has been developing a theory of gift giving since the 1970's as an alternative theory of communication and language as based in gift giving, seen as the unilateral satisfaction of needs. With the Center for the Study of the Gift Economy she recently organized and sponsored two international women's conferences. Vaughan has edited a collection of essays on the gift economy and is author of a children's book, *Mother Nature's Children* (1999). She has three daughters and lives part time in Italy.

Christine Woodrow is Head of Early Childhood Programs at the University of Western Sydney. In addition to her extensive experience in teacher education, she has had significant involvement in early childhood policy and curriculum development for early childhood education and care at a state and national level, including a 2 year term as Chair of the National Advisory Council on Childcare, providing advice on policy and strategic direction to the Federal government. She has held many positions on the boards of management of early childhood services, curriculum committees and state policy think tanks. Her current research activities include a focus on leadership, the impact of corporatisation of childcare and constructions of the child in early childhood policy, and she is participating in a 9 country study of professionalism in early childhood contexts.

Foreword

Early childhood education is a field that more recently than most fields in education has become professionalized, unionized, state-regulated, and subject to heavy intervention. In a clear and obvious historical sense 'the baby', 'the infant', 'the toddler', 'the preschooler', 'the child' has been an object of study for a range of educational theorists from well before the Enlightenment but with Descartes and Rousseau and those that followed them—Montessori, Freud, Piaget, Skinner, Mead, Kohlberg, Ariès, Donaldson to choose only a very few names from a long lineage—the question 'what is the child?' became at one a political, economic, historical and psychological issue. There are now huge, growing and complex literatures on cognitive development, moral development, children agency, children's rights, children's literature and all aspects of early childhood education. One could argue that the field of early childhood was an accepted legitimate field of inquiry well before the professionalization of early childhood education and its incorporation into universities as a specialist field within colleges of education. Today early childhood education is seen as a crucial area of intervention and research. The U.S. Department of Education sponsors and carries out research in early childhood education in the following areas: Assessment; Brain Development; Curriculum and Partnership; Curriculum; Ensuring Quality; Equity and Excellence; Family Involvement; Language and Literacy; Professional Development; School Readiness and Pre-Kindergarten; Second Language Learning; Technology; Inclusion; Early Intervention; Disability Specific; Special Needs.[1] Some of this research overlaps with other fields of research in education; some of it is early childhood specific; and much of it is medicalized. The focus of other research centers on reading or other forms of achievement. All, to a very large degree, rely on sets of philosophical assumptions about the child and about childhood and most of these are part of the protected unexamined metaphysical theoretical core that is never touched, acknowledged or revisited by research projects that take aspects of the notion of the child for granted.

After Ariès' (1962) path-breaking book *Centuries of Childhood* demonstrated how the notions of the child and childhood are culturally and historically constructed, there was an explosion of interest in 'childhood' and claims and counter-claims concerning the extent to which 'childhood' differs across cultures and ages. At the same time the older modernist and foundational views of the child and childhood came up for reexamination through the lenses of a myriad of critical approaches in psychoanalysis, critical pedagogy, critical psychology, feminism, critical sociology,

[1] See http://www.ed.gov/offices/OERI/ECI/hottopics.html. See also research at the National Center for Early Development & Learning (NCEDL), which 'focuses on enhancing the cognitive, social and emotional development of children from birth through age eight' at http://www.fpg.unc.edu/~ncedl/pages/research.cfm.

and poststructuralism. As the editors indicate in their introduction to this volume devoted to early childhood education it 'does not seek to, nor pretend to, provide a particular paradigm for education in early childhood' and they go on to say 'the topic belies a singular definition, especially where such definition is underscored by the heartless world of market exchange or any sense of preparation of young children for economic utility.'

What is particularly encouraging by this set of essays is that they are all critical—critical of dominant discourses and paradigms; critical of modernity and foundationalism; critical of normalization policies; critical of commercialization; critical of developmental theory; critical of the modernist theory-practice binary. And they adopt the critical apparatus and approaches from feminist theory and from the work of Foucault, Deleuze and Guattari, Lyotard and Derrida. They bring to bear these critical approaches on practices and policies of early childhood education in Australia, Sweden, New Zealand, France and elsewhere. They also provide arguments, analyses, new approaches in philosophy and ethics, and new forms of resistance that begins the critical task of reformulating early childhood education and the philosophy of the child.

MICHAEL A. PETERS
University of Illinois at Urbana-Champaign

Introduction

SANDY FARQUHAR & PETER FITZSIMONS
University of Auckland

The term 'early childhood education' refers to the theory and practice of educating young children. It also incorporates the education of adults about young children, particularly in the field of teacher education. The early childhood discourse has emerged in large part from a range of theorists in developmental psychology, with empirical observations and supervised *practicum* providing a means of applying theory to practice. Increasing numbers of children enrolled in early childhood education programmes might be interpreted merely in terms of changing employment patterns in Western economies. However, intensified government involvement in educational institutions and increasing standardisation of curricula suggest that education during early childhood has taken on a new social and political significance.

Contributors to this volume came together in the belief that early childhood education may benefit from an attitude of critical self-reflection in areas such as: childhood identity; critiques of the social sciences in defining 'the child'; theories of knowledge that seek certainty in a world of postmodern and often confusing difference; ethical issues in the relation to child, family and economy; standardisation and commodification of education; and the social formation of knowledge, truth, and even rationality. The intention was not to reject the current focus of early childhood education, but to engage in philosophical inquiry into the nature of the discourse from diverse perspectives outside the traditional realm of developmental psychology and related pedagogies, and to examine prevailing narratives that reify the world of early childhood education.

The notion of narrative is not new to early childhood: young children love to listen to stories, tell stories and create new selves in dramatic and imaginative play. As adults we listen to and observe children in their stories and relationships. Within narrative, education can be seen to be concerned with developing life stories, with individuals and communities making sense of actions and events by telling stories. In other words, narrative has the function of giving explanations of actions and events. Educational discourses inform and are informed by a variety of narratives that shape and guide how we think about children; how strategies, plans and policies are developed; how we educate educators; and how we teach children. Contemporary theories of narrative promote interpretive process and continual reciprocity, providing a framework in which human existence is rendered meaningful (Ricoeur, 1992).

Within the spirit of open-ended conversation and unfolding narrative, contributors to this special issue adopt a variety of perspectives on early childhood that enliven the debates and augment the possibilities for philosophy of education. While Froebel, Pestalozzi and Montessori have traditionally provided a rich ground for early childhood theory and practice, the authors in this collection represent a growing number of researchers, philosophers and teachers who are extending the philosophical parameters of the early childhood discourse with recourse to a variety of philosophical thinkers. To emphasise narrative is to keep alive the spirit of tentativeness, pluralism, inclusiveness, otherness and contingency in the face of encroachment by regulatory, outcomes-based, or market paradigms that neither emphasise nor provide for self-critical expression.

Our contributors are from vastly different geographic boundaries (England, the United States, Finland, France, Sweden, Australia and New Zealand); what they share in common is a preparedness to question what counts as received wisdom in early childhood education theory and practice, and a preference to acknowledge the complex and unique creations that are our children. This collection presents a strong argument for the importance of pluralism in examining different paradigms, so that any historical version of childhood may be acknowledged in its reflection of particular economic and community expectations. The rich and varied interpretations presented here, and the preparedness of our authors to step back from traditional narratives of early childhood, accord young children the unique respect they deserve, with implications for curriculum, pedagogy and policy.

Marking out the territory of paradigmatic difference, Peter Moss addresses the emergence of a dominant discourse in early childhood education and its lack of engagement with other paradigms. He argues that the absence of dialogue impoverishes early childhood, arguing the place for an agonistic pluralism to promote debate between incommensurate discourses and for a willingness to explore the possibility of common ground, or at least a curiosity about other perspectives. Moss recognises the disparate perspectives of foundationalist and post-foundationalist paradigms, although hope is held for mutual exploration by at least 'some members from some camps'. The chapter issues a challenge for those engaged in the field to extend the horizons of their own paradigms to incorporate the perspective of others: a fitting challenge for education, although one not to be taken lightly, especially in view of the historical and political setting of early childhood education.

Continuing the idea of paradigm, Eila Estola and Genevieve Vaughan introduce two 'contradictory but complementary' notions—the gift paradigm and the exchange paradigm as interpretations of the interactions that characterise early childhood education. The authors argue a strong connection between the gift paradigm and unilateral giving involved in mothering, advocating against the heartless world of market exchange as the dominant discursive mode for education. Their chapter explores the gift giving aspects of Froebel's and Montessori's philosophy and the new guidelines for early childhood education in Finland. The authors see the gift paradigm grounded in diverse documents and practices of early childhood education, and advocate for its wider application as a programme for social change and for engagement with early childhood education as an ethical enterprise.

Liselott Borgnon explores conceptions of the self in early childhood, offering a critique of developmentalism as definitive of the child, approaching early childhood education through the imagery of surfing. The chapter is relevant to contemporary post-structural discourse in early education, playing with new and creative configurations of the child subject through an understanding of Deleuze and some interesting metaphors associated with territory, weightlessness, and movement. When associated with the imagery of the child as learner-walker, Borgnon troubles the practices of calculating and organizing the child's physical progress, stepping out from the linearity of progress, and playing with freedom as a form of weightlessness.

Although focussing on teacher education in Sweden, Hillevi Lenz Taguchi's analysis of the dichotomy between theory and practice is applicable to the positioning of early childhood education across Western economies generally. The author challenges current practice to incorporate the perspective of the Other in a fresh and appealing way with recourse to student teacher narratives. She explores the transformation of teacher education programmes from academic vocational training, and upgrading the value of practice and the more 'feminine' aspects of learning. Adopting a poststructural perspective, the author steers us away from the idea of uncovering essential and fundamentally unchangeable human traits, preferring instead the idea that such understandings are contextualised through language. Through the mechanism of deconstructive talks, the author shows how student teachers are invited to reconstitute their experience with ethical attention to the Other—an important reformulation in the pre-school child's speaking, knowing and cooperative meaning-making.

Liane Mozère follows the conceptualizations of Foucault, and Deleuze and Guattari, in interrogating the notion of 'normal' in relation to the development of young children and exploring the deeper functions of language for children. Drawing on her own extended empirical research in crèches of Paris, Mozère distances herself from the societies of control typified by developmental and cognitive psychology in early childhood, preferring instead to focus on often ignored corporal, sensory, and non-verbal (as well as verbal) realms where she sees the most vivid manifestations of desire. Deligny's 'lines of wandering' allow for the emergence of a new narrative for young children's desire, and a recognition of the competence of the female staff members engaged with them.

As a New Zealand early childhood academic, Andrew Gibbons posits a metanarrative crisis within early childhood education, critically engaging with the idea of play as a process rather than a product, arguing that the treatment of play as a technology for the production of competence renders even the process itself as a product. His chapter draws strongly on the work of Lyotard and Foucault to portray the young child as governed within and by 'play as process', problematising the educator's role and promoting a broad critical perspective on assumptions that underpin educational concerns, rather than an unquestioning acceptance of process as the dominant narrative.

The final chapter by Christine Woodrow and Frances Press from Australia argues a strong relationship between the way a community constructs the notion of childhood and the practices and policies of that community. They explore the positioning of the child in historical, contemporary and emerging trends in Australian early childhood education and care, advising caution about the prevalence of a commercialised view of childhood that accompanies the increasing trend towards privatised provision of services. Drawing on the experiences and practices of early childhood pedagogues and policy actors both in Australia and overseas the authors posit an alternative construction of the child as citizen and the possibility of the early childhood field as a site for the practice of democracy.

It is with some excitement and extreme satisfaction then that we bring together here this diverse group of academic theorists, empirical researchers, teachers and writers to focus specifically on philosophical issues in early childhood education. This volume does not seek to, nor pretend to, provide a particular paradigm for education in early childhood, since as is well illustrated by the articles herein, the topic belies a singular definition, especially where such definition is underscored by the heartless world of market exchange or any sense of preparation of young children for economic utility. The enterprise resembles more an investigative smorgas-bord, or in artistic terms perhaps a collage of perspectives that enrich explanations of childhood, of young children's education, and of the institutions in which such endeavour occurs. Problematising the emergence of a dominant discourse in early childhood throughout Western systems of education, this collection valorises difference and perspective in early childhood, leaving room for otherness, and for the deep realms of being that children inhabit.

Reference

Ricoeur, P. (1992) *Oneself as Another*, K. Blamey, trans. (Chicago, University of Chicago Press).

1
Meetings Across the Paradigmatic Divide

PETER MOSS

University of London

The Rise of a Dominant Discourse ...

Early childhood education and care has risen up the policy agenda both of national governments and international organisations (such as the European Union, the Organisation for Economic Cooperation and Development and the World Bank). There has been an increase in investment, an expansion of services and an assertion of the importance of early childhood education for economic and social goals. This has been accompanied by the increasing dominance of a particular discourse about early childhood education in the English-speaking world, but also to a considerable extent elsewhere. It is an Anglo-American discourse spoken in the English language, and broadcast globally through the English-language outputs of researchers and international organisations. It is an example of what Santos (2004) refers to as 'hegemonic globalisation' that is 'the successful globalisation of a particular local and culturally-specific discourse to the point that it makes universal truth claims and "localises" all rival discourses' (p. 149).

The discourse has a distinct (and English) vocabulary: words like 'development', 'quality', 'readiness for school', 'best practice', 'benchmark' and 'outcomes' figure prominently. It draws heavily on a few disciplinary perspectives, notably child development and economics. It privileges instrumental rationality and technical practice, its prime questions being 'what are the outcomes?' and 'what works?' In doing so it sets up a binary opposition between process and outcome. It is inscribed with certain values and assumptions, for example certainty and linear progress, objectivity and universality. It understands the child as a knowledge reproducer and a redemptive agent, who can be the means of resolving many societal problems if only the correct technologies are applied at the right time ('early intervention'), and early childhood services as enclosures for the delivery of these technologies.

The reasons for the increasing dominance of this discourse, including its connection with the emergence since the 1970s of neo-liberalism and advanced liberalism as increasingly dominant economic and political regimes, have been considered elsewhere (Dahlberg & Moss, 2005). For the purposes of this article, however, it is important to add that the discourse is located within the paradigm of modernity, or more precisely the paradigm of a particular form of modernity, since it has been argued that modernity is not unitary; rather it contains different traditions (Hardt & Negri, 2001; Santos, 1995; Toulmin, 1990).[1] One tradition is emancipatory, placing high value on democracy, equality, difference and scepticism. But another, in which the Anglo-American early childhood discourse is situated, has been highly regulatory, foregrounding order, control and certitude and privileging a particular concept of reason and knowledge: an instrumental, calculating and totalising reason and a scientific knowledge that is unified and claims to reveal an objective and universal truth about humanity, history and nature. This tradition is inscribed with Cartesian, Hegelian and positivist epistemologies that assume, *inter alia*, 'the historical progress of man towards absolute knowledge and freedom ... [the possibility] to measure, represent, predict, and control knowledge of the social world; ... [and] a knowing, disinterested, rational subject who can uncover "objective" knowledge' (St. Pierre & Pillow, 2000, p. 6). Bloch (1992) argues that United States early childhood work, whether in publications, conferences or universities, has been tied to 'largely positivist and political-analytic paradigms in theory and method' (p. 4), which are based on a set of assumptions including universal, decontextualised theories, a belief that the social world exists as a system of separable variables and the distinction between theory and practice.

... and Other Discourses

Yet the situation in early childhood education today is more complex and fluid than this introduction might suggest. Certainly, policy makers both from national governments and international organisations, responding to increased political interest in early childhood, adopt a remarkably similar narrative, based on the dominant discourse I have outlined. A small number of studies, many of which emanate from very local experiences with highly disadvantaged children in the United States, are continually generalised and recycled to suggest that early intervention applying scientific knowledge will provide effective and efficient solutions to a range of social problems.

Yet over the last 15 years or so an increasing number of other discourses can be heard within early childhood education, which question, resist and trouble the dominant discourse. One source of these other discourses is a widening interest in what have been termed postfoundational ideas (Ninnes and Mehta, 2004), including postmodernisms, poststructualisms and postcolonialisms,[2] representing a very different paradigm. This paradigm challenges the basic tenets, or foundations, of the paradigm of regulatory modernity: the stable and coherent self, the transparency of language, the rationality of humans, the ability of reason to overcome conflicts between truth, power and knowledge and that freedom involves obeying rational laws (Flax, 1990).

Increasing numbers of scholars and others in the early childhood field have begun working with postfoundational ideas, in many countries including the United States. The first conference of the Reconceptualist group took place at the University of Wisconsin-Madison as far back as 1991, and has since been an annual event, attracting participants from a number of countries; the 13th international conference on reconceptualizing early childhood education returned to Madison in 2005, the previous conference having taken place in Oslo. There is a large and growing literature exploring the application of postfoundational ideas to early childhood education and at least one journal in the field—*Contemporary Issues in Early Childhood*—that is dedicated to 'exploring new and alternative perspectives' and welcomes submissions in areas including poststructuralist, postmodern and postcolonial approaches, queer theory, sociology of childhood, and alternative viewpoints of child development.

These and other developments have problematised most of the values, assumptions and understandings of the dominant early childhood discourse, with its foundational paradigm. Some examples of this process are outlined below.

- Child development has been contextualised and positioned as 'a paradigmatically modern discipline arising at a time of commitments to narratives of truth, objectivity, science and reason' (Burman, 1994, p. 18), its knowledge linked to power and its role in governing children explored. Fendler (2001) has argued that 'the interweaving of developmental psychology, efficiency and behaviourism in educational curricula becomes a technology of normalization [that I call developmentality] ... a current pattern of power in which the self disciplines the self' (p. 120).
- Developing this critique of developmentality, Fendler (ibid.) has shown how well established practices, such as 'developmentally appropriate practice', 'whole child education' and 'interactive pedagogy' contribute to processes of subjectification, in particular the creation of the child as a subject of neo-liberalism privileging flexibility and response-ability.
- The 'essential' child, the truth of whom can be discovered through science, must now contend with the socially constructed child, while the early childhood centre has similarly been reconceptualised as socially constructed: 'from a social constructionist perspective [early childhood institutions], as well as our images of what a child is, can be and should be, must be seen as the social construction of a community of human agents, originating through our active interaction with other people and with society (Dahlberg, Moss & Pence, 1999, p. 62).
- Postcolonial theories have also been used to critique constructions of the child, in particular by child development: '[T]he work of postcolonial scholars can be used to explain reasons for the consideration of child as colonizing construct ... First, and most easily related to the child, Bhabha (1996) discusses the production of the "other" (p. 37) through a colonial discourse generated by creating knowledge about the "other" through surveillance. The colonizing discourse creates a "subject people" (p. 37), who are described as lacking and in need of control by those who have generated the knowledge' (Canella and Viruru, 2004, p. 84).
- Quality, a key concept in the dominant discourse, has been deconstructed and shown to be paradigmatic and value-laden rather than self-evident and necessary: 'the concept of quality in relation to early childhood institutions is irretrievably modernist, it is part of the Cartesian dream of certainty and the Enlightenment's ambition for Progress and Truth. It is about a search for definitive and universal criteria, certainty and order—or it is about nothing. Working with complexity, values, diversity, subjectivity, multiple perspectives and temporal and spatial context means taking another position which understands the world in a different postmodern way' (Dahlberg *et al.*, 1999, p. 105).

• The technical practice and instrumental rationality embodied in the dominant discourse have been problematised as features of a long-term and more general process, which in recent years has gathered pace: draining political and ethical practice from a series of social issues and replacing them with technical practice. Apple (2004) describes in his study of curriculum how 'most advanced corporate societies seem to transform their ethical, political and aesthetic questions, for instance, into engineering problems. Profound conflict between opposing ideological and moral positions is translated into puzzles to be solved by the technical expertise that is maximised by the cultural apparatus' (p. 111). The possibility of making ethics and politics first practice in early childhood education has been explored, with particular attention given to postmodern ethics, an ethics of care and the ethics of an encounter, and to minor or minority politics (Dahlberg & Moss, 2005).

Influential in this work have been the writings of Continental European philosophers and social thinkers, not surprising given that the 'most persistent feature of [20th century] continental philosophy, through all its multiple manifestations, is a commitment to the questioning of foundations' (Kearney, 1994, p. 2). Today, it is possible to find references in early childhood literature to the likes of Derrida, Deleuze and Levinas. But most commonly cited is Michel Foucault, with his work on dominant discourses, power relations, including the exercise and effects of disciplinary power, and governmentality increasingly applied to the early childhood field.

Having set the scene briefly, with the attendant risk of over-simplification, I want to devote the rest of this article to questions that concern and intrigue me in equal measure and that are provoked by these parallel developments: the increasing hegemony of a particular discourse, accompanied by a vigorous growth of counter-discourses. Given a shared field of interest, early childhood, what relationship do these parallel developments have with each other, and what relationships could they have? Is it possible for them to engage in some form of productive dialogue? Or are they incommensurable, making any attempt at dialogue futile?

One Field, Many Camps

It seems to me that the situation that is emerging in early childhood is troubling. The field may be occupied by many camps, but these camps are grouped together on different sides of a divide, from where each gets very different perspectives: the divide is paradigmatic, separating modernist and postfoundational perspectives. The former espouses 'the modern idea of truth as reflective of nature ... [and] that the conflict of interpretations can be mediated or resolved in such a way as to provide a single coherent theory which corresponds to the way things are' (Babich, Bergoffen & Glynn, 1995, p. 1); while the latter adopts 'postmodern (Nietzschean) questions of interpretation, valuation, and perspectivalism ... [and] an infinitely interpretable reality where diverse, divergent, complementary, contradictory, and incommensurable interpretations contest each other' (ibid.). For the former, early childhood education is progressing inexorably to its apotheosis, based on the increasing ability of modern science to provide indisputable evidence of what works. While for the latter, early childhood education offers the prospect of infinite possibilities informed by local knowledge and provisional truths.

Each side has little to do with each other. This is an instance of what Babich has called 'incommensurate discourses', where paradigmatic difference gives limited scope for communication: statements that are clear and coherent within one discursive formation may not be intelligible within another (Foucault, 1972). Communication is restricted because the modernists do not recognise paradigm, or rather take their paradigm and its assumptions and values for granted; while the postfoundationalists recognise paradigm but see little virtue in the paradigm of modernity or at least have made the choice not to situate themselves within that paradigm. The one group therefore see no choice to make, the other has made a choice that involves situating themselves beyond modernity. Communications issued from one group of camps are dismissed by the other as invalid, unintelligible, uninteresting or incredible.

Does this relationship matter? Is it not the role of the postfoundationalists to develop alternative discourses and critical thinking, rather than fraternise with those with whom they appear to have nothing in common? And shouldn't modernists focus their attentions on what they believe in, the production of true knowledge? I think it does matter. The absence of dialogue and debate impoverishes early childhood and weakens democratic politics. 'Mainstream' policy and practice are isolated from an important source of new and different thought, while a dominant discourse is given too much uncritical space and increasingly undermines democracy by the process of depoliticisation already mentioned. Rather than such a discourse being regarded as a perspective privileging certain interests, it comes to be regarded as the only true account, the only questions being about the most effective methods of implementation.

In this situation, policy and practice choices are reduced to narrow technical questions of the 'what works?' variety. What Cherryholmes (1988) terms 'vulgar pragmatism' ('what is true and valued is what works in terms of what exists' (p. 178)) excludes 'critical pragmatism' (which 'continually involves making epistemological, ethical and aesthetic choices and translating them into discourse-practices' (p. 179)). Typically, there is no recognition by policy makers, or among most practitioners or those who educate them, of the paradigmatic nature of discourse and no discussion of or explanation for selecting either a paradigm or a particular discourse within that paradigm. In many years in the early childhood field, including much cross-national work, I cannot recall seeing a national or international policy document that recognises the existence of paradigm or acknowledges that there are different perspectives, understandings and answers available with which to frame policy, provision and practice. This is a stultifying state of affairs—or so it seems to me.

To expect anything different might be considered naïve. After all, it might be argued, politics and policy today is dominated by particular linked discourses—economic neo-liberalism partnered politically by what has been termed advanced liberalism (Rose, 1999)—inscribed with the values and assumptions of regulatory modernity. These linked discourses both place greater responsibility on the autonomous subject while introducing new techniques of government through the tenets and practices of new managerialism, the loyal lieutenant of advanced and neo-liberalism that 'proclaims itself the universally applicable solution to problems of inefficiency, incompetence and chaos' (Clarke, 1998, p. 174). In the circumstances, it might be thought that the best that can be envisaged is for those situating themselves in the postfoundational paradigm either to continue their work in isolation from the dominant paradigm, in monastic seclusion, or to conduct a sort of guerrilla warfare of dissidence which hardly registers in its impact.

Agonistic Pluralism

The prospect of engaging politically may be daunting and even a touch naïve, but I believe it is at least worth attempting. Not only does the dominance of one paradigm and one discourse impoverish democracy, but it also marginalises post-foundationalism, confining the increasing opus of work to a critical ghetto and denying any possibility of change. In this respect I agree with Halpin (2003) when he argues for the importance of utopian thinking that goes beyond simply critique:

> [Thomas] More did not write Utopia merely to stimulate the intelligence, least of all simply to amuse, but to challenge the social order of his time and to provide a fresh way of thinking about the direction of social change ... [U]topianism in education, and elsewhere for that matter, can perform the function of being a catalyst for social change, and in ways that social criticism on its own cannot. For only when the latter is expressed in terms of concrete suggestions for improvement—which is the way of most utopias—is it capable of performing this task. (p. 55)

By seeking political engagement, I am not proposing an exercise in Habermasian communicative ethics, with its search for consensus. Rather I am interested in the possibility of engagement in the political through what Mouffe (2000) terms 'agonistic pluralism'. Mouffe's starting point is 'the dimension of antagonism that is inherent in human relations, antagonism that can take many forms ... [and an understanding] that 'politics' consists in domesticating hostility and in trying to defuse the potential antagonism that exists in human relations' (p. 101). For the central question in democratic politics 'is not how to arrive at consensus without exclusion, since this would imply the eradication of the political ... [but how] to construct the 'them' in such a way that it is no longer perceived as an enemy to be destroyed, but as an 'adversary', that is somebody whose ideas we combat but whose right to defend them we do not put into question' (pp. 101–102). The fact that people from different camps may come together as adversaries does not mean that there can never be common ground: '[Agonistic pluralism does not mean] that adversaries can never cease to disagree ... Compromises are, of course, possible; they are part and parcel of politics; but they should be seen as temporary respites in an ongoing confrontation' (p. 102). She sums up by distinguishing between antagonism, agonism and the Habermasian concept of 'deliberative democracy':

Antagonism is struggle between enemies, while *agonism* is struggle between adversaries. We can therefore reformulate our problem by saying that envisaged from the perspective of 'agonistic pluralism' the aim of democratic politics is to transform *antagonism* into *agonism*. This requires providing channels through which collective passions will be given ways to express themselves over issues which, while allowing enough possibility for identification, will not construct the opponent as an enemy but as an adversary. An important difference with the model of 'deliberative democracy' is that for 'agonistic pluralism', the prime task of democratic politics is not to eliminate passions from the sphere of the public, in order to render a rational consensus possible, but to mobilize those passions towards democratic designs. (pp. 102–103; original emphasis)

I agree with Mouffe that a politics of agonistic pluralism is a condition for democracy. It recognises and legitimates conflict arising from different interests, values and perspectives: it does not give up on or deny profound differences of perspective. It also seems to me that it might provide a framework for thinking about how to bring some people located in different paradigms and working with different discourses into some form of engagement without requiring domination by one camp or a phoney consensus.

Creating Conditions for a Politics of Early Childhood

If agonistic politics provides a useful way of envisaging engagement between those situated within different paradigmatic positions or adopting different philosophical approaches, then to practice such politics will require, or at least benefit from, certain conditions.

Finding Common Ground

The recognition of conflict in politics does not mean that there need be no common ground. Talking generally, Mouffe refers to 'a shared adhesion to the ethico-political principles of liberal democracy: liberty and equality' (p. 102) whilst recognising there will be disagreement about the meaning and implementation of those principles. Such principles might similarly play a part in the narrower politics of early childhood education (or education more generally) that brought adherents of different perspectives into agonistic relationship.

It may also be necessary to identify some other common ground. This might involve—if not an outright acceptance of paradigm—at least a willingness to accept the possibility for the sake of argument, without requiring participants to renounce adherence to their particular paradigm; recognition of the possibility that there may be a variety of productive answers to the same question—and, of course, a range of different critical questions in the first place; and a willingness to explore the relationship between the universal and the particular on the basis that both have a role to play in early childhood education (while at the same time accepting that there are different views about what those roles are). Engagement may also require a modicum of curiosity about other perspectives, a desire to dialogue 'not as an exchange but as a process of transformation where you lose absolutely the possibility of controlling the final result' (Rinaldi, 2005, p. 184), and a consequent openness to explore, discuss and reflect.

An agonistic politics of early childhood education will not, therefore, be for everyone. Yet these conditions would not preclude developing an agonistic politics that attracts at least some occupying different positions in the field. Despite my attempt to emphasis multiplicity, my metaphor of camps on either side of a divide runs the risk of implying an absolute opposition and dualism—between two homogeneous groups—that distorts what I think is the actual situation. There is considerable diversity within the camps on each side of the divide, which itself is not a total barrier: there are crossing places and observation points. Postfoundationalists are generally understanding of, if not necessarily sympathetic to, foundationalist perspectives; some might concede that these perspectives can contribute to what Santos describes as 'local knowledge created through argumentative discourse' (1995, p. 37). Similarly, some positivists are aware of and understand postfoundational positions. There is even some movement between camps, in particular some foundationalists being drawn to understand more about the perspectives of postfoundationalists (in the realm of physical sciences, it is scientists themselves who have taken the lead in problematising the previously dominant Newtonian paradigm and have 'precipitated a profound epistemological reflection on scientific knowledge' (ibid., p. 20)). Given wide enough recognition of the importance of engagement and drawing on work by political scientists such as Mouffe, then new and productive relationships may emerge and flourish between at least some members drawn from some camps.

Finding Arenas for Engagement

If early childhood is to be a field where some members of different camps engage together in an agonistic politics, then we need to create arenas where such politics can take place. These can take many forms: in seminars, conferences, journals and other media, which might provide space for political argumentation; on courses, which might start by introducing students to the idea of paradigm; and in early childhood services themselves, where the question of paradigm and perspective can be introduced into the practice of what has been termed 'minor politics'. Various forms of documentary method—by which practice is made visible in various ways (e.g. written notes, video and audio recordings, children's work) and hence subject to interpretation, reflection, dialogue and valuation—provide one method for conducting agonistic minor politics in services themselves; examples from early childhood education include the video-based work of Tobin, Wu and Davidson (1989) and Hansen and Jensen (2004), pedagogical documentation as developed in Reggio Emilia (Dahlberg *et al.*, 1999; Rinaldi, 2005), and learning stories as developed in New Zealand (Carr, Jones & Lee, 2005).

How to reach politicians, policy makers and the wider public? This is harder to imagine. But perhaps, in the first place, postfoundationalists need to be willing to muster and present their perspectives in various public arenas—in response to official consultations, before parliamentary committees and similar official review bodies, in responses to the media. At the very least, politicians, policy makers and the media should be left with no excuse for believing that there is only one perspective on early childhood education, only one narrative to be told. The argument needs to be made cogently and rigorously that there is not one self evident direction to take, based on objective scientific knowledge and irrefutable evidence, but many possibilities, each based on different knowledge and perspectives: even the clearest fact has no meaning without interpretation.

One facet of this line of argument is that postfoundationalism does not give rise only to abstract concepts and theories and to criticism of what exists. It can also be applied, being productive of policy and practice that can be recognised by all as worthy of serious attention. Such examples already exist. The early childhood services in Reggio Emilia have attracted worldwide interest and admiration, one centre even being described as the 'best nursery in the world' by the American magazine *Newsweek* in 1991.[3] The pedagogical practice of Reggio has been interpreted as located in:

> ... a philosophical perspective which in many respects seems ... postmodern ... [S]ome of the elements of that practice, understanding and perspective [include]: choosing to adopt a social constructionist approach; challenging and deconstructing dominant discourses; ... rejecting the prescription of rules, goals, methods and standards, and in so doing risking uncertainty and complexity; having the courage to think for themselves in constructing new discourses, and in so doing daring to make the choice of understanding the child as a rich child, a child of infinite capabilities, a child born with a hundred languages; building a new pedagogical project, fore-grounding relationships and encounters, dialogue and negotiation, reflection and critical thinking; border crossing disciplines and perspectives, replacing either/or positions with an and/also openness; and understanding the contex-tualised and dynamic nature of pedagogical practice which problematizes the idea of a transferable 'programme'. (Dahlberg *et al.*, 1999, p. 122)[4]

Reggio also provides other examples of the application of postfoundational ideas. Through its use of pedagogical documentation, already referred to, it shows how evaluation can be understood as meaning making and making a judgement of value, so providing an alternative to the modernist concept of quality, where evaluation is understood as conformity to norm through the application of universal and stable criteria. Moreover, its theory and practise of the 'pedagogy of listening', it has been argued, reveals how ethics can be the starting point for practice in early childhood education, specifically the ethics of an encounter (Dahlberg & Moss, 2005).

Reggio's theory and practice have influenced early childhood education in many parts of the world, although the risk always exists that the theory and practice will be reinterpreted within a modernist paradigm. The problem here it seems to me is not interpretation *per se*, since there is no stable technical programme labelled Reggio that can be exported and directly applied: as Rinaldi (2005) observes

'Reggio itself is an interpretation of Reggio' (p. 197). Rather the problem is to take Reggio out of one paradigm and attempt to apply it to another, and in so doing deny its difference—a case of otherness being grasped and made into the same, which is a major risk of postfoundational thought and practice engaging with the dominant discourse.

One part of the world where Reggio has had a major influence is Sweden, apparent in government policy, the education of teachers and the networks of pre-schools linked to the Reggio Institute in Stockholm, engaged in co-constructive dialogue. Postfoundational thinkers have also begun to influence practice and research, not only Foucault but also Derrida and Deleuze (Dahlberg & Moss, 2005). MacNaughton (2005), working in Australia, has shown how Foucauldian theory can play an important part in the professional development of early childhood educators, providing vivid examples of these workers applying this body of theory in their everyday practice.

These and other examples demonstrate, in the most immediate of ways, how postfoundational ideas open up a variety of knowledge and a wide range of choices. They make early childhood education a highly contestable field. And they strengthen the hand of those on the modernist side of the divide who would like to engage in agonistic politics.

Intelligibility and Bugbears

One criticism of postfoundational work is that it is difficult to comprehend, hence by implication impeding the chances of agonistic politics. This issue of intelligibility is faced head-on by St. Pierre (2000), responding to a paper by Constas (1998). Constas notes that 'the field of educational enquiry finds itself in a state of transition caused by the increased activity and debates related to postmodernism' (p. 36), but finds it difficult to comprehend postmodernism in the context of educational research. He refers to 'the elusive nature of postmodernism' (p. 36) and seeks to get at its 'essential qualities' (p. 40), and 'to identify unifying elements' (p. 36). Frustrated by the ill-defined nature of postmodernism, he asks those who 'reject outright the very attempt to define postmodernism in a simplified scheme' to organise their responses into an 'intelligible set of assertions that encourages constructive dialogue about the nature of postmodern inquiry' (p. 41).

St. Pierre, in her riposte entitled 'The Call for Intelligibility in Postmodern Research', puts forward several reasons why Constas's request is not as simple as it seems. She raises the problem of how statements are discourse-specific, making sense within one discourse but not in another, and refers also to what Britzman (1995) calls 'the limits of intelligibility', the boundary 'where thought stops what it cannot bear to know, what it must shut out to think as it does' (p. 156). To cross the boundary 'we must make the intelligible appear against a backdrop of emptiness and deny the necessity. We must think that what exists is far from filling all possible spaces' (Foucault, 1997, pp. 39–40).

St. Pierre goes on to suggest that a more interesting question than 'what is postmodern educational research?' would be:

> How does one learn to hear and 'understand' a statement made within a different structure of intelligibility? At the least, this question shifts prevailing attitudes by assuming that the burden of intelligibility lies as much with the reader as with the writer, a position contrary to that of those who chide postmodernism for 'deliberate obfuscation over clarification' (Constas, 1998, p. 38). For some reason, these readers expect postmodernism to be readily accessible and coherent within a structure it works against. (St. Pierre, 2000, p. 25)

St. Pierre in turn chides Constas for not doing his homework, discussing and critiquing an approach without studying the philosophy that produces it:

> Postmodern analyses have been available—and elaborated in the detail Constas and others desire—for decades. Postmodern educators ... have explained their work for years. Thus, I do not believe that those who have only cursorily examined postmodernism should accuse those who have studied 'the original literature' of being unclear, incoherent, and unintelligible. (p. 26)

St. Pierre seems to me to identify some important issues that need to be on the table if an agonistic politics is to go anywhere. All involved need to be aware and think about how to become available to intelligibility, given the 'limits of intelligibility'. All involved need to be prepared to put time and effort into reading, no simple matter in times when space to read, think and discuss are squeezed by the relentless demands of managerial governance, whose interest resides in producing predictable outcomes and not appreciating any new perspectives that put a spanner in the inexorable process of delivery. Yet as someone who came rather late in life to appreciation of paradigmatic difference, finding this a rewarding but difficult task, I wonder if there is not room for people who can facilitate intelligibility, providing guidance on reading, being ready to discuss what is threatening, difficult to grasp or plain impenetrable: in short, to act as interpreters between people coming together from different paradigmatic positions.

One of their roles, but not their's alone, is to confront some common misunderstandings about different paradigms, which left unattended grow into bugbears, providing false grounds for not engaging. For instance, to question foundationalism does not mean giving way to despair, paralysis, nihilism, apoliticism or irresponsibility, but instead opens up to 'possibilities for different worlds that might, perhaps, not be so cruel to so many people' (St. Pierre & Willow, 2000, p. 3). Postfoundationalism does not reject scientific attitudes and methods, instrumental reason and value-neutral objectivity—no more than it rejects the opus of child development—but rather treats them as claims, not truths; partial and specific to particular discourses (Usher, Bryant and Johnston, 1997). Nor, to take a third and common misunderstanding, does postfoundationalism mean surrendering to an 'anything goes' relativism. Quite the contrary, discussions of what might be termed postfoundational ethics— such as Bauman's (1993) postmodern ethics, feminist writing on an ethics of care (for example, Tronto, 1993; Sevenhuijsen, 1999) or Levinas's oeuvre on an ethics of an encounter—place much greater ethical responsibility on each of us to make contextualised judgements and not to fall back on blanket moral codes. For if there is 'no absolute truth to which every instance can be compared for its truth-value, if truth is instead multiple and contextual, then the call for ethical practice shifts from grand, sweeping statements about truth and justice to engagements with specific, complex problems that do not have generalizable solutions' (St. Pierre, 2000, p. 25).

What Subjects for Agonistic Politics?

To get into the way of agonistic politics, to start the dialogic ball rolling, thought needs to be given to subjects that are important when viewed from within different paradigms and where the possibility of finding some compromises, provisional areas of agreement, is readily apparent. In other words, we should start where the prospects for a successful meeting seem most promising. Let me offer an example as one of a number of possibilities: the evaluation of early childhood education.

All concerned in the field might well agree that this was important—and a shared recognition of the importance of a subject might be added to the earlier conditions for political engagement. But there are disagreements about the meaning of evaluation and the desirability and feasibility of seeking an objective and definitive evaluation. I have already mentioned the problematisation of quality from a postmodern perspective, which has proposed another concept of evaluation: meaning making (Dahlberg *et al.*, 1999). The former purports to be a statement of fact, the latter a judgement of value; the former claims to be objective knowledge based on expert reason and offering closure, the latter a subjective perspective contingent on context and values and at best the means for arriving at some provisional agreement or compromise.

From a personal political and ethical perspective, I am drawn to meaning making. It seems to me to form part of how early childhood institutions might be (re)concep-tualised as, first and foremost, 'loci of ethical practices' (Readings, 1996, p. 161) and sites for the democratic practice of minority politics (Rose, 1999). It also provides one means for disrupting what seems to me a dangerous consequence of the increasing institutionalisation of childhood: within the context of a regulatory modernity, the ever increasing governing of the child through a highly instrumental rationality and the application of ever more powerful human technologies, in the hope that it is possible to ameliorate the results of chronic structural problems without needing to address the problems themselves.

At the same time, meaning making is very demanding, far more so than working with the concept of quality. With quality, you have closure when the norm is attained; then you can say you have a 'quality' early childhood service or programme. With meaning making you have a 'researching' or 'reflective' service; you never arrive at an ending, you are always in the middle, for ever deepening understanding, researching processes, constructing new knowledge, reworking the relationship of a service to its ever changing context. With 'quality', learning is acquiring the skills to work with a particular tool (such as a rating scale) or programme. With meaning making, the use of pedagogical documentation is a continuous and rigorous learning process, with 'a lot of experimenting as well as a lot of interpretive work on the part of the pedagogue, a lot of dialogue with other pedagogues in which multiple perspectives can be introduced' (Dahlberg *et al.*, 1999, p. 149).

Meaning making requires very exacting conditions: an educated, committed and reflective workforce; support from wise counsellors such as the *pedagogistas* in Reggio Emilia who work closely with small groups of educators; an organisation that values and prioritises pedagogical documentation; close and participatory relationships between children, parents and educators, but also other citizens; being at ease with critical and argumentative dialogue; and sustained local political trust, support and engagement combined with decentralisation giving space for local practice and evaluation. In most places such conditions are far from being met. In much of the English-speaking world, for example, early childhood education and care includes large swathes of under-resourced 'childcare' services, often competing with each other in market conditions; combined with nursery education or kindergarten provision that is subject to increasingly strong regulation through prescriptive curricula, testing and inspection systems in order to ensure they produce children who are ready for school. The concept and practice of meaning making is not likely to work well in such conditions; to legislate for meaning making would not only be a contradiction in terms, but would also be a disservice to many children who would be left without the modicum of protection offered by quality with its attendant norms.

Given these conditions, rather than setting up a complete opposition between quality and meaning making, it may be more useful to think of different relationships between these approaches: between more technical and normative approaches and more participatory and contextualised approaches. Most countries are likely to have some national (or, in federal states, regional) system of regulation, including some or all of an array of standards, curricula, specified goals and inspection methods. But how detailed, prescriptive and normative a system is can vary, so leaving greater or lesser space for other more localised and participatory systems for evaluating and practicing pedagogical work. Not only is the relationship dependent on current context, it is also open to change over time, as conditions change (for example, increasing the feasibility of meaning making) and as the relationship between local and central, diversity and coherence changes.

An agonistic politics of evaluation could start by understanding the different concepts of evaluation, and their paradigmatic settings; the tools available for practicing different concepts; and the conditions needed to enable particular concepts and tools. This might then lead to argumentation about the relationship between different concepts in a particular spatial context (country, region, local authority), both in the current context and as an ideal to be striven for. As I have already indicated, not everyone in the early childhood field will choose to engage in this form of politics. But those who do will be participating in what Santos (1995) has termed 'argumentative discourse'. From the perspective of the modernist participant, this discourse might be seen as a search for scientific truth, while for the postfoundational participant, this discourse can only take place in an 'interpretive community' which in turn creates local and emancipatory knowledge. But in reality, the fact of engagement will produce shifting, often hybrid understandings which can inform and shape policy and practice—even new concepts of evaluation, since 'quality' and 'meaning making' do not constitute the sum total of approaches to evaluation.

Reasons for Hope

In the course of writing this article I came across work in another field of education— comparative education—which had many similarities to my own line of thought. Gorostiaga and Paulston (2004), writing about mapping diverse perspectives on school decentralization for an edited book titled *Reimagining Comparative Education*,

> ... choose to see a re-imagined comparative education *as an agonistic space of contested interpretations and negotiated realities* ... [W]e believe that the method of social mapping performed [in their study] has the potential of contributing to dialogues—as joint reflection and action—among different actors about research, policy and practice ... Opening space to include as many different positions as possible and uncovering textual inter-relations might well foster dialogue and better understanding among actors who see themselves occupying irreconcilable positions. (pp. 256, 278–279; emphasis added)

This piece offers yet another tool—social mapping—which might contribute to agonistic politics, and there is every reason to think that there are, or could be, many more.

The possibility, illustrated by this example, that similar discussions—about how to encompass within a shared political frame discourses generated by different paradigms—may be developing in other fields, providing inspiration and provocation both theoretically and in practice, is one cause for hope. Another cause is the increasing confidence and spread of other discourses in the early childhood field, which I have loosely described as postfoundational in paradigm. The hope, though, is not generated by regulatory modernity's assumption of linear and inevitable progress through finding the one true way. Rather, it lies in the possibility of a more dialogic, plural and democratic early childhood field, and more effective resistance to dominant, and stultifying, discourses: not the prospect of finding the one true way, but the possibility of finding many ways to many truths.

For me, the importance of such hope is summed up in these words of Popkewitz (2003), which also remind us of the paradigmatic legacy that many, now in various camps, share:

> The problematic of this essay is diagnostic, to show the contingency of the arrangement that we live and thus open up the possibilities of other ways of living ... To disturb the groundwork that makes the present possible is a form of resistance that makes possible other alternatives. My argument, however, should not be read as a critique of the attitude embodied in a cosmopolitan reason. The discussion is, I believe, framed in the Enlightenment's faith in reason and, in that sense, I am a 'child' of

the Enlightenment. But the discussion recognises, to borrow from Foucault, that reason is not a universal and that different modes of reason need to be called forth. (p. 56)

Notes

1. By paradigm I refer to an overarching system of ideas and beliefs by which people see and organize the world in a coherent way, a mindset for making sense of the world and our place in it. By discourse I refer to ways of naming things and talking about them. Dominant discourses—what Foucault refers to as 'regimes of truth'—exercise a decisive influence on specific practices by determining some things to be self-evident and realistic and rendering subjective perspectives into apparently objective truths. In so doing, they exclude other ways of understanding and interpreting the world. Discourses are constituted within paradigms, and share the ideas and beliefs of the paradigm.
2. The use of plurals here recognises the multiplicity of ideas subsumed under these headings. Schrift (1995) explains that 'poststructuralism is not a monolithic theory ... [but] a loose association of thinkers who draw from several shared sources' (p. 6). While St. Pierre (2000) comments that it is impossible to define postmodernism [or poststructuralism] in a simplified scheme since 'postmodernism *does not* and *cannot* provide essentializing answers to questions about its meaning' (p. 26: original emphasis).
3. Such language, and the thinking it represents, exemplifies a modern paradigm that finds credible the idea of universal and stable criteria.
4. The early childhood workers in Reggio Emilia have been cautious about identifying with postmodernism. Rinaldi (2005) comments that 'although Reggio may be postmodern in its perspectives, we are not for postmodernism, because 'isms' are risky. Because they simplify and lock you in prison again. Instead your freedom is to challenge ... Because to be postmodern means to challenge.' (p. 182).

References

Apple, M. (2004) *Ideology and Curriculum*, 3rd edn. (London, RoutledgeFalmer).

Babich, B., Bergoffen, D. & Glynn, S. (1995) On the Idea of Continental and Postmodern Perspectives in the Philosophy of Science, in: B. Babich, D. Bergoffen & S. Glynn (eds), *Continental and Postmodern Perspectives in the Philosophy of Science* (Aldershot, Avebury) pp. 1–7.

Bauman, Z. (1993) *Postmodern Ethics* (Oxford, Blackwell).

Bhabha, H. (1996) The Other Question, in: P. Mongia (ed.), *Contemporary Postcolonial Theory: A reader* (London, Arnold).

Bloch, M. (1992) Critical Perspectives on the Historical Relationship between Child Development and Early Childhood Education Research, in: S. Kessler and B. Swadener (eds), *Reconceptualizing the Early Childhood Curriculum: Beginning the dialogue.* (New York, Teachers College Press) pp. 3–20.

Britzman, D. P. (1995) Is There a Queer Pedagogy? Or, stop reading straight. *Educational Theory*, 45:2, pp. 151–165.

Burman, E. (1994) *Deconstructing Developmental Psychology* (London, Routledge).

Canella, G. S. & Viruru, R. (2004) *Childhood and Postcolonialization: Power, education, and contemporary practice* (New York, RoutledgeFalmer).

Carr, M., Jones, C. & Lee, W. (2005) Beyond Listening: Can assessment practice play a part?, in: A. Clark, A. T. Kjørholt & P. Moss (eds), *Beyond Listening: Children's perspectives on early childhood services* (Bristol, Policy Press) pp. 129–150.

Cherryholmes, C. H. (1988) *Power and Criticism: Post-structural investigations in education* (New York, Teachers College Press).

Clarke, J. (1998) Thriving on Chaos? Mangerialisation and the welfare state, in: J. Carter (ed.), *Postmodernity and the Fragmentation of Welfare* (London, Routledge) pp. 171–186.

Constas, M. A. (1998) Deciphering Postmodern Educational Research, *Educational Researcher*, 27:9, pp. 36–42.

Dahlberg, G. & Moss, P. (2005) *Ethics and Politics in Early Childhood Education* (London, Routledge).

Dahlberg, G., Moss, P. & Pence, A. (1999) *Beyond Quality in Early Childhood Education and Care: Postmodern perspectives* (London, Falmer).

Fendler, L. (2001) Educating Flexible Souls, in: K. Hultqvist & G. Dahlberg (eds), *Governing the Child in the New Millennium* (London, RoutledgeFalmer) pp. 119–142.

Flax, J. (1990) Postmodernism and Gender Relations in Feminist theory, in: L. J. Nicholson (ed.), *Feminism/Postmodernism.* (New York, Routledge) pp. 39–62.

Foucault, M. (1972) *The Archaeology of Knowledge and the Discourse of Language* (New York, Pantheon Books).

Foucault, M. (1997) Friendship as a Way of Life (R. de Ceecaty, J. Danet & J. le Bitoux, Interviewers), in: *Ethics: subjectivity and truth* (New York, New Press) pp. 135–140.

Gorostiaga, J. & Paulston, R. (2004) Mapping Diverse Perspectives on School Decentralisation: The global debate and the case of Argentina, in: P. Ninnes & S. Mehta (eds) *Re-Imagining Comparative Education: Post-foundational ideas and applications for critical times* (London, Routledge) pp. 255–280.

Halpin, D. (2003) *Hope and Education* (London, Routledge).

Hansen, H. K. & Jensen, J. J. (2004) A Study of Understandings in Care and Pedagogical Practice: Experiences using the Sophos model in cross national studies. Available at http://www.ioe.ac.uk/tcru/carework.htm

Hardt, M. & Negri, A. (2001) *Empire* (Cambridge, MA, Harvard University Press).

Kearney, R. (1994) Introduction, in: R. Kearney (ed.), *Continental Philosophy in the 20th Century* (London, Routledge) pp. 1–4.

MacNaughton, G. (2005) *Doing Foucault in Early Childhood Studies: Applying poststructural ideas* (London, RoutledgeFalmer).

Mouffe, C. (2000) *The Democratic Paradox* (London, Verso).

Ninnes, P. & Mehta, S. (2004) Introduction: Re-imagining comparative education, in: P. Ninnes and S. Mehta (eds), *Re-Imagining Comparative Education: Postfoundational ideas and applications for critical times* (London, RoutledgeFalmer) pp. vii–xiii.

Popkewitz, T. (2003) Governing the Child and Pedagogicalisation of the Parent: A historical excursus into the present, in: M. Bloch, K. Holmlund, I. Moqvist and T. Popkewitz (eds), *Governing Children, Families and Education: Restructuring the welfare state* (New York, Palgrave MacMillan) pp. 35–61.

Readings, B. (1996) *The University in Ruins* (Cambridge, MA, Harvard University Press).

Rinaldi, C. (2005) *In Dialogue with Reggio Emilia* (London, Routledge).

Rose, N. (1999) *Powers of Freedom: Reframing political thought* (Cambridge, Cambridge University Press).

Santos, B. de S. (1995) *Towards a New Common Sense: Law, science and politics in the paradigmatic transition* (London, Routledge).

Santos, B. de S. (2004). Interview with Boaventura de Sousa Santos, *Globalisation, Societies and Education*, 2:2, pp. 147–160.

Schrift, A. D. (1995) *Nietzsche's French Legacy: A genealogy of poststructuralism* (New York, Routledge).

Sevenhuijsen. S. (1999) *Citizenship and the Ethics of Care: Feminist considerations on justice, morality and politics* (London, Routledge).

St. Pierre, E. A. (2000) The Call for Intelligibility in Postmodern Educational Research, *Educational Researcher*, 29:5, pp. 25–28.

St. Pierre, E. A. and Pillow, W. S. (2000) Introduction: Inquiry among the ruins, in: E. A. St. Pierre & S. W. Pillow (eds), *Working the Ruins: Feminist poststructural theory and methods in education* (New York, Routledge).

Tobin, J., Wu, D. Y. & Davidson, D. H. (1989) *Pre-School in Three Cultures* (New Haven, CT, Yale University Press).

Toulmin, S. (1990) *Cosmopolis: The hidden agenda of modernity* (Chicago, IL, University of Chicago Press).

Tronto, J. (1993) Moral Boundaries: A political argument for the ethics of care (London, Routledge).

Usher, R., Bryant, I. & Johnston, R. (1997) *Adult Education and the Postmodern Challenge: Learning beyond the limits* (London, Routledge).

2

The Gift Paradigm in Early Childhood Education

GENEVIEVE VAUGHAN & EILA ESTOLA
Austin, Texas, USA; University of Oulu

Introduction

In order to understand the confusing and often tragic world in which we live, we may consider that there are two main paradigms or worldviews present in society today.[1] These are the gift paradigm and the exchange paradigm, each of which has its own logic and values.

In this chapter our main interest is in the gift paradigm in early childhood education.[2] We will first describe the notion of the gift paradigm in general and then give examples of the gift paradigm in three educational texts from three centuries. After that we give examples of how the gift paradigm is or can be present in daily practices. Our deeper aim however, is to promote the recognition of gift-giving in general at all the levels of our society.

The gift paradigm and the exchange paradigm are 'logically contradictory, but also complementary. One is visible, the other invisible; one highly valued, the other undervalued. One is connected with men; the other with women' (Vaughan, 1991, p. 84). These paradigms may also be seen in terms of Marx's structure/superstructure distinction, where deep economic patterns determine ideological superstructures. The logic of the exchange paradigm requires an equal payment for each need-satisfying good, while the gift paradigm contains a transitive logic by which a giver unilaterally satisfies the need of a receiver and thereby establishes bonds of mutuality and trust. The exchange logic is ego-oriented while the gift logic is other-oriented. The return payment in fact, cancels the gift and turns the value-attributing mechanism back from the receiver towards the giver. The exchange paradigm and the values of ego-orientation that are associated with it are widespread today as the principle of the market, and they influence all our thinking. The gift paradigm continues to exist in mothering young children (who cannot exchange an equivalent for their care), and exists invisibly in many other areas of life, but is discredited and concealed by the exchange paradigm. In spite of this difficult context, the logic and the practice of gift giving continue to give rise to the values of care and community. Moreover, those practicing the gift paradigm actually give to those practicing the exchange paradigm, ameliorating otherwise unliveable conditions and providing the personal and systemic rewards that motivate the system.

From the point of view of the gift paradigm, women's free labor in the home is a gift to the economy of exchange and the market. Because the two paradigms coexist, but one of them is invisible, the gifts given to the institutions of exchange are often a paradoxical way of colluding with oppression.

The structures of exchange appear to coincide with those of reason itself, and they are often unwittingly internalized, even by those who continue to practice the gift paradigm. Vaughan's hypothesis is that the exchange paradigm is actually harmful, producing patriarchy and domination. The gift paradigm is 'humanizing', fertile and creative, and should be brought forward, while the exchange paradigm should be diminished (Vaughan, 1997).

We use the concepts of 'voice' and 'metaphor' as methodological tools to describe how the gift paradigm is present in educational texts and practices. In terms of 'voice', playgroups and classrooms are multivoiced places (Elbaz-Luwisch, Moen and Gudmundsdottir, 2002). Some of the voices are more audible than others. We will look at the gift paradigm simultaneously with the exchange paradigm in order to pay attention to the fact that the voice of exchange is becoming so strong that it almost silences the other voices. One reason for the invisibility of the gift paradigm can be found in Bakhtin (1981) who separates the authoritative discourse from internally persuasive discourse. The former 'demands that we acknowledge it, that we make it our own; it binds us, quite independent of any power it might have to persuade us internally' (p. 342). Freema Elbaz-Luwisch (2005) points out that we often recognize the authoritative discourse by who is speaking. In present times the exchange paradigm often frames education as business. This means that the speaking person, the voice of authoritative discourse, is male, since men own the majority of the world's property (Kailo, 2004). Women form the majority of those who work with small children as care-givers and teachers but often work under male administration. Those who speak in the voice of gift-giving are mainly women, and we are writing this article from a feminist perspective.

The concept of 'metaphor' supports our understanding of the relationships between the gift giving practice and its verbal forms. George Lakoff and Mark Johnson extended the study of metaphors to cognitive theory, arguing that our thinking has material ground (Lakoff & Johnson, 1980). Metaphors are thick descriptions, short stories, which have their roots in practice. They are devices for making sense of one phenomenon in terms of another and are fundamental to our understanding. Metaphors guide our thinking and our way of seeing the world, making some features obvious and visible while simultaneously concealing some other features. They are like stories that never tell the whole story but have a moral message to transmit. Metaphors in education are tools for thinking; they are bridges between the known and the unknown; they facilitate communication and focus the gaze on certain aspects rather than others.

What is the Gift Paradigm?

The gift paradigm is a way of looking at mothering and other instances of unilateral gift giving that have not been recognized as such. Jacques Derrida (1992) says that unilateral gift giving is impossible. He reasons that if the gift is recognized as such it is no longer unilateral, since recognition functions as a pay back. However it is clear that this consequence can only take place where gift giving is unusual. If it is commonplace no special merit or recognition is connected with doing it. Mothers commonly do a great deal of gift giving, which is unrecognized. In fact, mothering can be seen as a mode of distribution (presently confined to the 'private sphere') in which goods are given directly to needs. Recognizing this would resolve Derrida's paradox by providing unilateral acts of care with a context in which they are not unusual. It would also make it advisable to revise the first page of economics textbooks, to include gift giving in the category 'economic'. Vaughan's contention is that a superstructure of values and ideas already accompanies the hidden economic structure of unilateral gift giving. These are the values of other orientation and altruism, which are presently attacked and eroded by the market ideology of the rights and privileges of ego oriented '*homo economicus*'.

The logic of unilateral gift giving is simpler than the logic of exchange but it carries with it implications that differ from those of exchange. By unilaterally satisfying the needs of another we attribute value to the other by implication. That is, if we did not give value to the other we would not want to satisfy his or her need. On the other hand if we give to the other only to receive an equivalent value in exchange, we satisfy our own need by means of the other. In this way, we imply our own value, while the other is valuable to us only instrumentally, as a means. Gift giving is other oriented while exchange is ego oriented. Unilateral egalitarian gift giving establishes bonds of community between the giver and receiver by which each can recognize the existence and importance of the other. In contrast, exchange creates adversarial relations as each person tries to get more out of the transaction than the other, instrumentalizing her or him. Gift giving is primarily qualitative while exchange is quantitative. It is cooperative where exchange is conflictual. Gift giving is changeable however, and when it is used for ego-oriented purposes, it does transform into an exchange. This can happen for example, when gifts are given in non-egalitarian contexts, for purposes of manipulation and domination or self-aggrandizement.

The two paradigms are in conflict, a circumstance which causes many people to embrace the values of the dominant exchange paradigm even when they are actually doing a great deal of gift giving. Thus the caregiver of AIDS patients may say, 'I do it because I get so much back', framing her or his care-giving as exchange, when in fact any positive gift giving brings with it a certain amount of satisfaction and sense of meaningfulness in a world rendered meaningless by manipulation and the market. The idea of gift giving as communication (com-muni-cation: *muni-* Latin 'gifts') allows us to see how meaning in language and meaning in life are connected through satisfying needs (Vaughan, 1997).

From the point of view of the gift paradigm, language satisfies communicative needs arising from the historical, physical and mental situations in which the interlocutors find themselves. Words can be seen as verbal gifts, which take the place of material gifts in establishing mutual community-forming communicative relations. The market, which is based on exchange, can be seen as an aberrant communicative or semiotic mechanism. It sorts the more from the less valuable, and validates the more valuable while eliminating what is free. The market is a sorting mechanism dividing free gifts from exchange values, categorizing owners as superior to the propertyless, and categorizing all human beings as valuable according to the kinds and quantities of property they can afford (Vaughan, 1997; 2003).

If the market functions as an aberrant communicative mechanism and human beings are basically sign processing, communicative animals, it follows that we humans would be deeply influenced in our thinking by the market. Moreover, the gift giving which we learn with our caregivers and which is a source of positive communication and community, becomes the substance of profit: the gifts of unpaid labor given by workers to capitalists, embedded in the free housework of women, the free and low cost labor of third world nations, and free and low cost natural resources. In fact gift-givers give to exchangers and to the market where the gifts are ignored, renamed, and cancelled by self-validating market processes. Globalization itself is a process in which the market is taking over and making commodities out of many previously free gifts such as water and bio-diverse indigenous species of plants and animals (cf. Korten, 1995; Shiva, 1997; 2000; Latouche, 2004).

The two paradigms lead us towards two ways of being in the world, one of which is consonant with the market and motivates us towards domination and aggrandizement, while the other promotes other orientation, cooperation and community. The market requires agents with ego-oriented motivations in order to create investment and capital accumulation. At the same time it destroys community and limits the quality of life for many of its participants while condemning to poverty all those without access to salaried labor. Those who practice the gift paradigm are vulnerable to exploitation by the market, although the gift paradigm can be seen as the source of the values of care that make life possible and worth living. The two paradigms are locked into a paradoxical parasitic relationship that disqualifies gift giving and over values exchange. Ethically however, the gift paradigm is superior to the exchange paradigm, and is in fact the direction all of us should take to create a better world. Market excesses, which cannot be curbed effectively within the exchange paradigm itself, have created situations of grave ecological imbalance, and continue to give rise to wars for local and global domination. The gift paradigm, by giving attention to needs at all levels and beyond the market concept of 'effective demand', motivates us towards the well being of others and a peaceful future for the planet, without prioritizing the profit motive. It seems evident to the authors that promoting the gift paradigm in early childhood will not only allow children to develop better values in their individual lives but will help to validate those values in the society at large so that choices and policies can become more consciously life-affirming.

The Concept of the Gift Paradigm in Early Childhood Education

Education, in its broad and general meaning, starts almost immediately when the baby is born, first in nurturing and caring, later in many other ways. Issues arising from the gift paradigm and the exchange paradigm begin to influence children at an early age. In order to succeed in the market people need to be educated into the market logic and values when they are young. Gender is an issue here because girls are encouraged to be unilaterally gift giving like the mother, while boys are taught that they must have a gender identity that is not like the mother, not gift giving. This non-mothering identity is then privileged over and above the mothering identity, even by the mothers themselves (Vaughan, 1997; 2002; 2004b).

By requiring an equal exchange and cancelling gift-giving, the market provides an area of life appropriate for a non-nurturing identity. In order to socialize everyone into a market-based society, the values of self-interest, equal exchange, competition, acquisition (of knowledge or objects) and domination are promoted. The perspective of the gift paradigm is cancelled, made to seem impractical, irrational and relegated to the unconscious. The perspective of exchange combines with the institutions and values of patriarchy, encouraging a race to the 'top', to dominance through power and possessions.

Many paradoxes accompany the coexistence of the two paradigms. The gift paradigm gives to its 'other', which is the exchange paradigm, but remains unrecognized in the process, so that the exchange paradigm appears to stand alone. Though its values may be heartless and cause much suffering, the market seems to dictate the only possible world. Those who wish to educate their children in another way seem to have no alternative, because if the children cannot succeed in the market as adults, they will not be able to survive. A both/and way out of this seemingly either/ or situation needs to be found. The gift paradigm has to be salvaged at the same time that the exchange paradigm is being taught, with the goal of finally phasing out the exchange paradigm and bringing forward the gift paradigm. In order to do this, the logic of gift giving and its values can be uncovered and validated where they already exist.

The continuity between mothering and later forms of gift giving, or social nurturing, can be recognized, as well as the connection between mothering and language. Young children are close to the gift economy because they have experienced it as receivers of what is to them free care. In fact the care is free to the children even if the caregivers are paid professionals. There are many qualitative aspects of care that are 'priceless' to the receiver, whatever the quantity of remuneration that is paid to the provider. The first harbingers of the exchange logic are perhaps the rewards and punishments for behaviors, introducing the idea of exchange by making children 'pay' for mistakes, and bestowing rewards for being 'good'.

A way out of the paradox could be facilitated also by recognizing and enhancing the gift paradigm aspects of the care giving and teaching professions. Children could then pass from the gift giving practiced by their mothers to environments in which gift giving would be consciously practiced and validated by teachers for the children and as a commitment of the teaching profession. Later as young adults, students could also be seen as the recipients and sharers of the gifts of knowledge transmitted by teachers and the society as a whole. In contrast at present, competition for jobs and consequently for high marks places students in adversarial relations with one other, typical of the market, so that the circulation of knowledge is halted by a kind of privatization. The gifts of knowledge are denatured, their need-satisfying characteristics altered and they are placed in the service not of humanity but of the military industrial complex. Students are required to become proficient in the kinds of knowledge that supports the economy.

The creation of scarcity by the market, taking wealth out of the economy by cornering it in the hands of the few, and by making such non-nurturing collective expenditures as the development and production of armaments, makes gift giving difficult, and thereby avoids competition between the (more satisfying and humane) gift paradigm and the dominant exchange paradigm. The mentality that legitimizes the social inequalities created by this artificial scarcity is developed by schools that frame education within the ego-oriented exchange paradigm.

A child can be supported to adopt gift-giving. Giving to some one who needs help and respecting the other person's view are two important aspects of learning empathy and other-orientation. A child who found a $20 bill at a harvesting party of a gift-oriented Montessori school in Kyle, Texas first tried to find the owner and finally put it in a box in which he was saving money to help people. The teacher enthusiastically validated these choices (Estrada, 2005).

On another occasion in the same school a three year-old asked a four year-old to play but the older boy said 'No'. Then the younger child started to threaten him: 'You are not my best friend; you are not going to my house'. To this the older one said 'You have to respect my "No". You should not be mad or saying those things to me. I have the right to say "No" '. Again the teacher supported the response (ibid.).

For young children, the experience of the gift paradigm continues even when their needs are being satisfied, not by the mother, but by a paid care provider. Children necessarily live in a gift economy because they are dependent on others for the satisfaction of their needs, and they cannot exchange an equivalent for what they receive. The caregivers thus have a choice to continue emphasizing gift giving, or to teach exchange, which seems to be the way of the 'real world'. The institutions to which the providers of care belong are structured by the exchange paradigm while mothercare or nurturing seems to be a very limited and specific experience. (In fact, patriarchy, the market and matriphobia have undermined mothercare as a key for the interpretation of the world.) Nevertheless motivations coming from the gift paradigm can be identified in teachers' subjective accounts of their own experience (Estola, 2004). Mothers, teachers and care providers can choose to emphasize and validate gift giving as a paradigm, which they intentionally communicate to the children, rather than promoting exchange.

The exchange paradigm includes such methods as rewards and punishment—credit or guilt and 'paying' for wrong-doing. The needs of others are considered instrumental to the satisfaction of one's own needs and desires. The gift paradigm promotes sensitivity to the needs of others and the validity and normality of satisfying them. Modeling gift giving and legitimating that model rather than the model of exchange-domination allows children to continue to imitate the mother and validate maternal logic. They can do this by taking turns with adults or other children in giving and receiving as well as in exploring a safe mother-world, a process by which they acquire experiential *data*, the gifts of experience.

Along with families and primary relationships, educational institutions are places where children are taught to adopt the main values and practices of the society in which they live. The exchange paradigm is the worldview that is being increasingly embraced by our society. For that reason, education is expected to be profitable, pay-back, similar to companies or factories. Education, day care centers and schools are expected to be cost efficient, and competitive. Human beings become instruments of exchange, and the highest value is offered for the 'best', the winner. The biggest investment is made in those who will provide the greatest quantifiable return, i.e., will be most 'economically productive' in the future. This discourse is highly individualistic, encouraging people to search primarily for their own good. There is little room for talking about education as a gift. The space for this discourse continues to exist primarily among those who do that need-satisfying other-oriented practice: the teachers.

The Gift Paradigm in the Texts of Early Childhood Education

The gift paradigm has existed in diverse forms through the western history of early childhood education, identifiable in the ideas of Friedrich Froebel (1782–1852) and Maria Montessori (1870–1952), and in the Curriculum of Early Childhood Education and Care in Finland since 2003. These are now explored in a series of three snapshots depicting the relationship between gift giving and early childhood education.

First, is the well-known term 'kindergarten' developed by Froebel and used for the first time in 1840 (Grue-Sørensen, 1961). 'Kindergarten' is a typical example of a metaphor emerging from the natural environment. Since metaphors feed the imaginary, they concretize abstract phenomena; so 'kindergarten' opens the door to the wider landscape of what educating young children is at its deepest. It suggests the picture of a gardener walking in the middle of growing flowers and taking care of them, watering and fertilizing them when necessary. Froebel belonged to the group of Romantic educational philosophers. He founded kindergartens using the ideas of Comenius, Rousseau and Pestalozzi, emphasising that education must start at an early age and that play is the most important method in education. Froebel's educational philosophy has been said to be very complicated and hard to understand but his practical ideas have expanded all over the world. He specified three toys that were to be given to the children as gifts. In Froebel's philosophy these gifts, a ball, a cube and a cylinder, had deep metaphysical meanings. He developed a system regarding the order in which these gifts were meant to be given to the children. There were also various forms of the gifts, for instance in different kinds of puzzles.

In the beginning Froebel educated his male friends and family members working with him. Later, when kindergartens had become more established and Froebel was able to recruit students outside his family and friends, he preferred women as kindergarten teachers. Part of his educational philosophy was his appreciation of women as teachers and educators. Froebel developed kindergartens to support education at home and although he thought that women have a special role in families, he stressed that both parents must be engaged in education. Froebel resisted the common understanding that women have a natural aptitude to raise children. On the contrary, he was convinced that women need to be educated for child raising and being mothers (Salminen & Salminen, 1986).

For Froebel, to care for others was as important as to be cared-for. In his book for mothers, *Mutter und Koselieder*, he emphasized that children need to learn to take care of animals in order to be able to take care of other people (Froebel, 1982). Froebel's entire philosophy can be interpreted as other-oriented, in that he was striving for the best for children. Froebel laid the foundation for future early childhood education by paying attention to the early years as a special period of life with its own characteristics. This can be understood as Froebel's gift to early childhood education.

The second snapshot depicts Maria Montessori who also had a strong influence on early childhood education. Her most famous book *Discovery of the Child* (1969) has been used in many countries. Montessori developed her pedagogy based on the positivistic paradigm. She studied medicine and is said to have been the first woman to finish a doctoral dissertation in medicine in Italy. The basic idea in Montessori pedagogy is to support children to do things by themselves. She argued that children need an environment suited to their own size, including items like furniture. She also developed a special program including learning materials designed to develop children's abilities and skills.

Though we might say it is the teacher's duty to prepare children for hard reality—that is, to prepare them for a non-nurturing world—the very attempt to satisfy this need for preparation is gift-based. Even when people do not have the idea of gift giving in mind, they practice it when honoring the needs of others. Thus Maria Montessori, in honoring the needs of children to explore and find their own ways, practices gift giving, even if it is not called that by name. Montessori pedagogy was also other oriented: she advised adults to forget their own preconceptions and let children follow their own developmental ways. For instance, Montessori noticed that children want to repeat many activities although adults might not see any sense in them. Montessori points out that teachers must be passive organizing only the environment, and not regarding success as their personal credit. Montessori pedagogy is strongly based on the conviction that adults must honor children's own worlds. This can be understood as appropriate to the gift paradigm because the adults have to satisfy the children's need for independence and autonomy. Moreover, the main aim is to support children and not to wait for thanks or obedience as 'paying-back'. We can also refer to Montessori's own example, which is a concrete example of the gift paradigm at work. She describes how her children learned to take care of the environment and then started to teach their own parents to do the same at home. In gift paradigm language, this can be understood as a gift from A (teacher) to B (children), from B (children) to C (parents), and from C (parents) to D (the living environment and neighbors).

The third snapshot of the gift paradigm in early childhood education comes from the Finnish *'National Curriculum Guidelines on Early Childhood Education and Care'* (2003/2004, hereafter referred to as NCG). The guidelines have been written according to the Convention of the Rights of the Child and the Finnish basic regulations and policy documents. They concern all the forms of publicly operated or supervised early childhood education. The Finnish model of early childhood education and care, called ECEC, is a multi-voiced concept with a background in the history of early childhood education. As Anna-Leena Välimäki (1998) has pointed out, Finnish early childhood education has roots in health, social welfare, labor and educational policy.

The guidelines express the cornerstone idea of Finnish early childhood education, which is the link between education and care. This very word 'care' appears in the name of the guidelines. This link implies that Finnish early childhood education should promote equality, the child's best interests and right to full development. The guidelines underline children's right to warm personal relationships and the general responsiveness of others to children's needs. In terms of the gift paradigm we could state that the idea of education as a gift is written in the guidelines. The guidelines also hold adults responsible for putting the values into practice in asserting that adults must 'act consciously in accordance with ethically and professionally sound principles' (NCG 2003/2004, p. 16).

The guidelines can be understood as messages from the politicians and administrators to the educators to direct their attention towards certain values and goals. The guidelines include several details that, with good reason, can be said to express the voice of gift giving. Generally speaking they all can be understood as other oriented without expectation of equivalent paying back. To take some examples: the guidelines contain the statement that they have been written in order to foster childhood and to underline the intrinsic value of childhood (NCG, 2003/2004, p. 14). This principle means that Finnish social, welfare and educational policy, do not discriminate against people according to their financial resources. Finland is known as one of the countries with approximately equal income distribution, with no extremely rich or extremely poor people. The state has a strong role in taking care of the weakest members of the society by income transfer and state and municipality paid services. From the 1970s this has meant in early education that both wealthy and poor families have had their children in the same day care centers and schools.

During recent years the voices of politicians have been changing, in a way understood here as silencing the voices of the gift paradigm. The newest cases are from the fall of 2004, when some politicians and officials questioned the right of every child to have a place in a day care center, because it was seen as too expensive. This debate was directed against mothers especially. The media told stories about how some mothers wanted to put their older children in day care centers although the mothers at the same time might be at home with a younger child. The right to a place in a day care center was not considered within a pedagogical framework, which could have allowed the discussion of education from the perspective of the child's needs. Since the gift paradigm promotes the consideration of needs, both of the children and of the mothers, this kind of development is troubling.

The guidelines advise educators to ensure that broad goals will be taken into account because they are meant 'to underline the intrinsic value of childhood, to foster childhood, and to help the child develop as a human being' (NCG, 2003/2004, p. 14). The three goals are: promotion of personal wellbeing; reinforcement of considerate behavior and action towards others; and a gradual build-up of autonomy. The guidelines give the following explanations for the goals:

> In promoting personal well-being, the focus is on respect for each child's individuality. This allows children to act and develop as their own unique personalities. Reinforcement of considerate behaviour and action towards others as an educational goal means that children learn to think of other

people and care about them. They think positively of themselves, other people, and other cultures and environments. ECEC contributes to providing conditions favourable for the creation of a good society and a common world. Gradual build-up of autonomy aims to help children to grow up into adults who are able to take care of themselves and people close to them and to make decisions and choices concerning their own lives. (NCG, 2003/2004, p. 14)

The three goals present a two-dimensional approach for ECEC: the educators have to take care of, on the one hand, the development of the individual person; and on the other hand, the individual as a member of the community. The emphasis in the guidelines on social goals and communities supports the gift paradigm. But having sophisticated aims does not mean that they are necessarily carried out in practice. Teachers can perceive children according to the exchange paradigm or the gift paradigm, although, as we have argued several times in this chapter, the voices of the exchange paradigm are becoming louder. That is why it is important to ask how to support children to grow up as caring persons who are able to feel empathy and behave in other-oriented ways according to the gift paradigm.

The word 'care' as used in ECEC is worth a comment. Although not stated explicitly, it seems obvious that 'care' has commonalities with the ethics of caring as 'a way of being in the world' (Noddings, 2001, p. 99). It also emphasizes the other-orientation, dialogical interaction and responsiveness to the other person's need: 'for some moments at least, we are receptive' (p. 99). Caring can be also connected with the social goals, which have been an inseparable part of the pedagogical aims and practices. It seems however, that the general ideology of individualism is claiming more space in a very insidious way. In her research, Tiilikka (2005) reveals contradictions in espousing both social and individual ideals. Mothers whose children were in day care centers emphasized that children were not allowed to injure the rights of others, and that children should take other people into account. However, the mothers did not talk about the concrete help and support of others, or about the wish that one should behave altruistically and sometimes do some things on the behalf of the other. Tiilikka concludes that educators should pay more attention to supporting children to help others.

The gift paradigm is evident in the guidelines document, but there is no assurance that it will become recognized and put into practice. To the contrary, there is a danger that the present over-valuation of the market and the exchange paradigm will tempt teachers and officials to ignore the voices of the gift paradigm.

The Gift paradigm in Daily practices of Early Childhood Education

Turn-taking

The gift paradigm emphasizes turn-taking instead of paying-back. The salient factor in turn-taking is that the child takes the adult as a model and imitates her, but this is not an exchange. When it is her turn, the child can imitate the adult's gift giving by becoming the agent, giving to the adult who takes the role of the recipient, but this is not conditional or manipulative; it is another unilateral gift, even if she or he is only playing (Vaughan, 1997).

Turn taking is reciprocal if the adult then imitates the child. However when one person makes her giving contingent upon the receiver's satisfying her need in return, the logic of the interaction becomes that of exchange. If the adult keeps manipulating and trying to exchange, to make the child behave 'properly' through rewards and punishments, the child may well imitate that model also and so start 'exchanging' earlier. Participating in the exchange interaction lays down patterns, which are repeated in other areas of life. For example, reprisal for a wrong that has been done to us, getting 'even', is a repetition of the pattern of equal exchange. By not requiring an equal payment but by looking from the meta level at the need which underlies an aggressive action, we can choose not to retaliate, and instead to implement the gift paradigm. That is, we can for-give the other person, acting according to the gift logic instead of the exchange logic (ibid. p. 97).

When children are small, both males and females identify with a primary care giver who is usually female. However, when they learn language, boy children discover they are in a gender category that is different from the care giving mother's category, even her opposite (Noddings, 1984). Since the most obvious characteristic of their mothers for young children is nurturing, it seems that the category that is opposite to mothering must be non-nurturing, not-giving (Vaughan, 1997; Ducat, 2004). Boys are encouraged to identify with male models, who are often distant and inaccessible and have undergone the same process of gender construction when they were growing up. The market, the exchange paradigm, patriarchy, and most of the institutions of society provide an environment, which validates this *artificially* non-nurturing identity. In fact if gift giving is such an important part of communication and community, there is very little that can serve as the content of a non-nurturing gender identity. Transposed gift patterns are thus invented, such as hitting, which, like nurturing touches the other but establishes a relation of dominance rather than a relation of mutuality and trust.

Exchanging blows and reprisals are an early form of exchange for children, but are usually never resolved even in adulthood and develop socially into attacks and counter attacks between individuals and between nations in violence and war. Addressing this issue in early childhood would be very important for changing society. If male children can be taught that they can and do also practice the unilateral gift paradigm, the harmful motivation towards competition, war and domination can be minimized (Ducat, 2004; Vaughan, 2004a). Humans beings are a species that uses gift giving to communicate and we are therefore all already nurturing beings (*homo donans* rather than only *homo sapiens*) but we are educating ourselves not to nurture (Vaughan, 1997). Educators can take this into account and help to restore the mothering gift paradigm by consciously teaching it to boys as well as to girls in early childhood.

The Gift Paradigm in Teachers' Stories and Educational Practices

In our research project on Finnish teachers' stories, many teachers described their work as 'serving others' (Estola, Erkkilä & Syrjälä, 2003). The serving idea can be a source of joy but it can also be a source of concerns and worries about how to deal with children.

One beginning teacher found similarities when comparing teaching and service jobs. There is the idea of gift giving as satisfying needs of the other when the teacher explains that if a teacher provides poor services, she is likely to be a poor teacher. The teacher tells a story about a ninth-grader who improved his mark by two units and concludes that it was probably the first time he had ever had a positive learning experience at school. The teacher tells how she was happy about the boy's positive learning experience and says that many things in teaching are more closely related to attitudes than learning facts and skills. Although the evidence is limited, it appears that the teacher's argumentation follows the idea of gift giving: to satisfy the child's needs without expecting 'paying back'.

Some of the teachers connected serving others with the idea of 'calling' or 'vocation'. This is easy to understand if we define 'calling' as something as practical as mothering: children call the adults to take care of them (van Manen, 1991). Although teaching is not equivalent to mothering, the similarities should not be underestimated either (Sikes, 1997). Teachers often describe their becoming a mother or father as a personal critical phase during which they learned a lot about being a teacher. Becoming a mother or father teaches us about the uniqueness of each child (Kelchtermans, 1993). This does not automatically mean that teachers adopt the gift paradigm when they become mothers or fathers especially because the gift paradigm is not appreciated in the society.

In this project a large majority of the teachers are women and they use words like 'love', 'trust', and 'caring' when describing their relationships with the children. Those words can be said to be part of the 'internally persuasive discourse' (Bakhtin 1981/1990, pp. 343–345) for the teachers. Some of the teachers say that they are worried about the current situation in which the administration wants them to do plans, assessments, curricula, and plans again, all of which means time away from the children. Teachers consider it important to listen to children's voices and needs, and do not consider education as a project of economic efficiency or competition. Rather, they see education as a long and slow process of interaction between a teacher and children. In contemporary society, this voice is often silenced, however, or considered old-fashioned. Teachers' stories can be interpreted as evidence of an other-oriented practice and expressions of the gift paradigm.

'Care' is a word commonly used by teachers, and can be interpreted in light of the gift paradigm. It is clear that the gift paradigm as expressed in teachers' stories is close to what Noddings (1984) calls 'caring' and what in her later book (Noddings, 1992) she presents as an alternative approach for schools. She classifies six categories in which caring can and should exist in education: caring for self; caring for the inner circle; caring for strangers and distant others; caring for ideas; caring for animals, plants and the earth; and caring for the human-made world. At first sight caring and the gift paradigm seem very similar. We see the relation between these two concepts as multiple and even complex. Although the ethics of caring is at the foundation of the gift paradigm, the gift paradigm is wider. The ethics of caring is especially concerned with the interaction, responsiveness and sensitivity in dyadic relationships. It has been developed as a complement to the ethics of justice. The gift paradigm has been developed as an alternative to the exchange paradigm. Vaughan (1991) has written about how gift paradigm challenges the ethics of justice: 'we do not need justice we need for-giving', she argues (p. 85). In the gift paradigm, the beginning is in the dyadic relationship, but the vision is how to construct the chain of givings: A gives to B and B to C and C to D etc. Especially when thinking about communication as a gift giving and about nature as a gift, it is easier to understand that the gift paradigm involves at least a common understanding of caring.

The receiver is as important as the giver in the gift paradigm. In order to complete the transaction, the receiver must creatively receive and use what has been given, or pass it on. While this does not constitute an obligation in the sense of 'paying back', the logical consequence of not using the gift transforms it away from its positive character and the gift is cancelled or wasted. The gift paradigm educates us towards other orientation, deriving 'ethical' behavior directly from the actions and paradigm we practice rather than trying to impose it upon people who have already been educated towards egotism and exchange.

Teachers do not always think or act according to the gift paradigm. Their daily practice takes place in the middle of various voices with which teachers are in a dialogue (Elbaz-Luwisch, 2005). Because the exchange paradigm is getting louder, it is not surprising that teachers behave according to the exchange paradigm. But teachers also often behave according to the gift paradigm, and that is important: the gift paradigm persists.

Young children are close to the gift paradigm because they are still being unilaterally mothered. Schools have had the paradoxical task of fitting children to the exchange paradigm while maintaining (or 'teaching') enough of the gift paradigm to make them 'good citizens'. They do this by giving and taking away gifts, nurturing, and closeness in order to impose behaviors. In other words, they use gifts as rewards and punishments, i.e. exchanges. Below are some practical ideas about how to promote the gift paradigm in early childhood education, with emphasis on the critical attitude needed towards all aspects of education.

A) THE ANALYSIS OF AIMS AND GOALS

As pointed out in the previous sections, the gift paradigm can be found in educational texts if we use a careful poststructural reading, which we have done by taking paying attention to gender and language. In fact, poststructural feminist research has pointed out that many concepts have gendered meanings. Hélène Cixous (1997) points out the gendered meaning of the gift that in the masculine context is not seen in terms of generosity.

Educators who want to promote the gift paradigm have to be sensitive about which aims and goals they emphasize in their curricula for children. We pointed out that voices of the gift paradigm echo in traditions of early childhood education. We also argued that the gift paradigm can be seen in National Curriculum Guidelines on Early Childhood Education and Care in Finland (2003/2004). At the same time there are voices of the exchange paradigm, which can easily silence the feminine voice of gift-giving and other orientation. For this reason it is a challenge to the teachers and other educators not only to read official aims and goals of education but also to be careful about which aims they want to emphasize.

B) THE METAPHORS

Since education is full of metaphors (starting from the word 'kindergarten'), educators should be careful when talking about early childhood education. Promoting the gift paradigm indicates a preference for concepts and metaphors that emerge from the gift paradigm and from mothering. It might be useful to ask oneself, 'Do I see education as competition or collaboration? Is education training for work or preparing for living a meaningful life?'

C) THE METHODS

There are signs that our present trend is back towards rigid modes of discipline, severe punishments and the adult's absolute authority. For instance there is a law in Finland that physical punishment is forbidden. This law is, however, questioned not only among the 'common people' but sometimes by so-called educational experts. Some of those experts advocate hard discipline for the children, especially those with behavioral problems. This is a paradox since those working with children and adolescents who have problems strongly argue that these young people have often had hard, even abusive, childhoods. What they have not had is love, hugs, smiles and empathy (Haapasalo 2000; Haapasalo & Aaltonen, 1999; Scannapieco & Connell-Carrick, 2005). In order to promote the gift paradigm, love, forgiveness and attachment are needed. Endless cycles of abuse and authoritarian excesses, disguised or overt, can be traced back to early childhood. At a general level, world leaders often embrace a hypermasculinized (Vaughan, 1997; Ducat, 2004) non-nurturing ideology that leads to aggression and counterattack, economic and military competition for hegemony, to the devastation of billions of lives and the destruction of the gifts of the global environment. Affirming the gift paradigm shows a way to peace that is already available, if we can validate and teach it.

D) LEARNING MATERIALS, TOYS AND EQUIPMENT

Play is the most important form of activity in early childhood. The research points out that children's games and play are gendered from the early years (Browne, 2004). However, often teachers are not aware that they themselves do not try to change this gender-based culture but instead they maintain it by guiding children according to cultural gender expectations. For this reason special attention should be paid to play corners, toys and playing materials. From the gift paradigm perspective, educators should be especially sensitive to supporting other-oriented play activities, like nurturing, caring, making food and other household work also for boys as well as girls.

It is important to talk about fairy tales as having to do with gift giving versus exchange, seen as a way to prepare children for the 'real world'. This transition from gift giving to exchange is visible in children's stories like Red Riding Hood (the child, who is taking gifts to the grandmother, is in danger of becoming food for the wolf) and in Hansel and Gretel (the free food of the witch's house contains the witch who wants to eat the children). Snow White is sent away by her cruel stepmother but receives the help of the dwarfs. Cinderella, enslaved to her sisters and stepmother (giving too many gifts) receives magic gifts from her fairy godmother that help her attract the prince.

The Finnish fairy tales by Tove Jansson about moomins are an excellent example of modern stories within the gift paradigm. The mother moomin is the person who is totally open-minded, who welcomes all the visitors, has enormous tolerance for difference and even manages to love an invisible child visible again. Although the moomin valley is a paradise-like place, it is not a paradise in the usual sense. The inhabitants, a miscellaneous group of characters, have all the human emotions and conflicts, although there is no war, they do not fight and they often manage to behave in other-oriented ways.

Conclusion

The gift paradigm, best seen as a program for social change, already exists in the logic of unilateral gift giving and communication. Revising our perspective towards gift giving and away from market exchange, we can envision a kind of education, which would help to cause a transition towards a society that could satisfy the needs of all. We could teach boys that they too can be nurturing like their mothers and teachers. We could encourage the identification of needs and the giving of care, and we could connect the idea of nature's abundance with the gift giving way. We are all mothered children, or we do not survive. We should encourage all children in the mothering way.

In its deepest sense, education is gift-giving. First, education is gift giving as a practice. It is what mothers and teachers frequently do with children. Second, education is gift giving at the level of a frame for understanding. If we talk about education as gift-giving, we give a verbal, symbolic name to the gift paradigm practice. By doing so, the words we use take on the positive character of metaphors, as tools for thinking, bridges between the known and unknown, focusing the gaze on certain aspects of behavior rather than others (Sumsion, 2002; Salo, 2003). The consideration of education as a gift includes a moral message of other-orientation in a small package. Applying the concept of the gift paradigm to education feeds maternal thinking in education (Ruddick, 1989; Naskali, 1998). When teachers talk about loving and caring about children or describe their work as 'serving others', 'fulfilling children's needs', these are important symbolic verbal messages to society that in teachers' work the gift paradigm has an important role.

In this article we have described the notion of the gift paradigm and given examples of how the gift paradigm can be found in the ideas of Friedrich Froebel, Maria Montessori and in the new Finnish guidelines on early childhood education and care. Since Finnish early childhood education has been strongly affected by both Froebel and Montessori the present guidelines echo their voices, too, and the existence of the gift paradigm in the Finnish guidelines is not surprising. Our 'findings' are based on 'reading differently', a method which is often used in feminist research. As a conclusion we argue that the gift paradigm is grounded in diverse documents and practices of early childhood education. We have also demonstrated how the exchange paradigm silences the voices of the gift paradigm. Finally, we aimed to promote the recognition of gift-giving in general at all the levels of our society. Our article is a step in that direction.

Acknowledgements

Our warm thanks to Dr. Kaarina Kailo for introducing us to each other and for her comments on an earlier version of this article.

Notes

1. The term 'paradigm' was introduced by Thomas Kuhn, regarding scientific thinking but has been broadened to mean a comprehensive, consistent and articulated worldview of any kind.
2. The vocabulary of early childhood education is very much culturally based. Nurseries, pre-schools, kindergartens, day care centers etc. have diverse meanings in various countries. In Finland there is no such difference but 'päiväkoti' (= day care center) is the word that is used for public, private, part-time and full-time day care for all children under the school age, which is seven years. Both the United States and Finland belong to the rich western countries and share many similarities. However, Finland as a Scandinavian country differs from the United States in many respects, not least in the way in which social and health policy as well as the comprehensive school system have been organized. For instance, in Finland every child has the right to early childhood services (see Kess, 2002). Children also start school at different ages, which means that the ages of children in early childhood education differ too.

References

Bakhtin, M. (1981/1990) *The Dialogic Imagination*, in: M. Holquist (ed.), *Four Essays by M. M. Bakhtin* (Austin, University of Texas Press).

Browne, N. (2004) *Gender Equity in the Early Years* (Open University Press, Glasgow).

Cixous, H. (1997) Sorties: Out and Out: Attacks/ways Out/Forays, in: A. D. Schrift (ed.), *The Logic of the Gift. Toward on Ethic Generosity* (London, Routledge), pp. 148–173.

Derrida, J. (1992) *Given Time: 1 Counterfeit Money*, P. Kamuf, trans. (Chicago, University of Chicago Press).

Ducat, S. (2004) *The Wimp Factor, Gender Gaps, Holy Wars and the Politics of Anxious Masculinity* (Boston, Beacon Press).

Elbaz-Luwisch, F. (2005) *Teachers' Voices: Storytelling and Possibility. The arts and practices of storytelling*. A volume in the series Issues in Curriculum Theory, Policy, and Research. I. Westbury and M. Osborne (eds) (Charlotte, NC, Information Age Publishing).

Elbaz-Luwisch, F., Moen, T. & Gudmundsdottir, S. (2002) The Multivoicedness of Classrooms: Bakhtin and narratives of teaching, in: R. Huttunen, H. L. T. Heikkinen & L. Syrjälä (eds), *Narrative Research. Voices of Teachers and Philosophers*, SoPhi 67, (Jyväskylä, University of Jyväskylä), pp. 197–218.

Estola, E. (2004) Education as a Gift, in: G. Vaughan (ed.), *The Gift/Il Dono: A feminist analysis*, Athanor, Semiotica, Filosofia, Arte, Letteratura, anno XV, 8, (Roma, Meltemi Editore), pp. 97–105.

Estola, E., Erkkilä, R. & Syrjälä, L. (2003) A Moral Voice of Vocation in Teachers' Narratives. *Teachers and Teaching: Theory and Practice*, 9:3, pp. 239–256.

Estrada, Ana Maria, (2005) Personal communication.

Froebel, F. (1982) *Mutter- und Koselieder* (Bad Neustadt a.d. Saale, Mitteldeutsche Verlagsgesellschaft).

Grue-Sørensen, K. (1961) *Kasvatuksen historia II. Pestalozzista nykyaikaan.* [History of education. From Pestalozzi to modern time, in Finnish] (Helsinki, WSOY).

Haapasalo, J. (2000) Väkivallan perintö: rikoksentekijöiden traumaattiset lapsuudenkokemukset [A Heritage of Violence: the traumatic childhood experiences of criminals, in Finnish] *Nuorisotutkimus* [the Finnish Journal of Youth Research], 20:4, pp. 3–17.

Haapasalo, J. & Aaltonen, T. (1999) Mothers' Abusive Childhood Predicts Child Abuse, *Child Abuse Review*, 8:4, pp. 231–250.

Kailo, K. (2004) Giving Back to the Gift Paradigm: Another worldview is possible, in: G. Vaughan (ed.), *The Gift/Il Dono: A feminist analysis*, Athanor, Semiotica, Filosofia, Arte, Letteratura, anno XV, 8, (Roma, Meltemi Editore) pp. 39–67.

Kelchtermans, G. (1993) Teachers and their Career Story: A biographical perspective on professional development, in: C. Day, J. Calderhead & P. Denicolo (eds), *Research on Teacher Thinking: Understanding professional development* (London, The Falmer Press) pp. 198–219.

Kess, H. (2002) The Child's Right to Early Childhood Services in Finland, in: L. K. S. Chan & E. J. Mellor (eds), *International Developments in Early Childhood Services.* (New York, Peter Lang) pp. 71–79.

Korten, D. (1995) *When Corporations Rule the World* (Berrett-Kohler, San Francisco).

Lakoff, G. & Johnson, M. (1980) *Metaphors We Live By* (Chicago, University of Chicago Press).

Latouche, S. (2004) *Altri Mondi, Altre Menti, Altrimenti: Oikonomia vernacolare e societa' conviviale* (Soveria Mannelli, Rubbettino Editore).

Montessori, M. (1969) *Lapsen salaisuus* [Discovery of the Child, in Finnish trans. J. A. Hollo] (Helsinki, Werner Söderström Osakeyhtiö).

Naskali, P. (1998) *Tyttö, äiti, kasvatus. Kohti feminiinistä kasvatusfilosofiaa.* [Girl, Mother, Education. Towards a feminine philosophy of education, in Finnish] Acta Universitatis Lapponiensis 18 (Rovaniemi, Lapin yliopisto).

National Curriculum Guidelines on Early Childhood Education and Care. (2003/2004) [referred 3.4.2005] available on line at: http://www.stakes.fi/varttua/english/e_vasu.pdf

Noddings, N. (1984) *Caring: AfFeminine approach to ethics and moral education* (Berkeley, University of California Press).

Noddings, N. (1992) *The Challenge to Care in Schools. An alternative approach to education* (New York, Teachers College Press).

Noddings, N. (2001) The Caring Teacher, in: V. Richardson (ed.), *Handbook of Research on Teaching*, 4th edn. (Washington, American Educational Research Association) pp. 99–105.

Ruddick, S. (1989) *Maternal Thinking. Toward a politics of peace* (Boston, Beacon Press).

Salminen, H. & Salminen, J. (1986) *Lastentarhatoiminta—osa lapsuuden historia.* [Kindergartens—Part of history of childhood, in Finnish] Mannerheimin Lastensuojeluliitto P17.

Salo, P. (2003) Lönar det sig att odla eller plocka pärlor i språket?—om metaforer i pedagogisk forskning, in Swedish. Paper presented in *Kasvatustieteen päivät*, Finland, Helsinki.

Scannapieco, M. & Connell-Carrick, K. (2005) *Understanding Child Maltreatment: An ecological and developmental perspective* (New York, Oxford University Press).

Shiva, V. (1997) *Biopiracy: The plunder of nature and knowledge* (Cambridge, MA, South End Press).

Shiva, V. (2000) *Stolen Harvest: The hijacking of the global food supply* (Cambridge, MA, South End Press).

Sikes, P. (1997) *Parents Who Teach. Stories from home and from school* (London, Cassell).

Sumsion, J. (2002) Becoming, Being and Unbecoming an Early Childhood Educator: A phenomenological case study of teacher attrition, *Teaching and Teacher Education*, 18:7, pp. 869–885.

Tiilikka, A. (2005) *Äitien kasvatuskäsityksiä ja arviointeja hyvästä päiväkotikasvatuksesta.* [Mothers' Conceptions of Education and Assessments of Good Day-Nursery Education, in Finnish]. Acta Universitatis Ouluensis, E76. (Oulu, University of Oulu).

Van Manen, M. (1991) *The Tact of Teaching. The meaning of pedagogical thoughtfulness* (Ontario, The Althouse Press).

Vaughan, G. (1991) The Gift Economy, *MS magazine*, May/June, pp. 84–85.

Vaughan, G. (1997) *For-Giving. A feminist criticism of exchange* (Austin, TX, Plain View Press).

Vaughan, G. (2002) Mothering, Communication and the Gifts of Language, in: E. Wyschogrod, J-J. Goux & E. Boynton (eds), *The Enigma of the Gift and Sacrifice* (New York, Forhdam University Press) pp. 91–113.

Vaughan, G. (2003) The Gift of the Gift in: S. Petrilli & P. Calefato (eds), *Logica, Dialogica, Ideologica* (Milano, Mimesis) pp. 337–348.

Vaughan, G. (2004a) Gift Giving and Exchange: Genders are economic identities and economies are based on gender, in: G. Vaughan (ed.), *The Gift/Il Dono: A feminist analysis*, Athanor Semiotica, Filosofia, Arte, Letteratura, anno XV, 8, (Roma, Meltemi Editore) pp. 15–38.

Vaughan, G. (2004b) Heterosexual Economics in: *A Radically Different Worldview is Possible*. DVD Series from Las Vegas Conference. (Austin, TX, The Center for the Study of the Gift Economy).

Välimäki, A-L. (1998) *Päivittäin. Lasten (päivä)hoitojärjestelyjen muotoutuminen varhaiskasvun ympäristönä suomalaisessa yhteiskunnassa 1800- ja 1900-luvulla.* [Every Day. The evolution of the children's (day)care system as an environment for early growth in Finnish society in the 19th and 20th centuries, in Finnish]. Acta Universitatis Ouluensis E31. (Oulu, University of Oulu).

3
Conceptions of the Self in Early Childhood: Territorializing identities

LISELOTT BORGNON
Institute of Education, Stockholm

Prologue

> Deterritorialization, and its obverse, reterritorialization, implicitly tie monadic thinking to the art of displacement and transformation ... Those who conceive of organic and inorganic matter from this point of view tend to be geophilosophers. Their activity 'slides' on the surface of the world, as on a wave. A 'surfer', the geophilosopher moves along the crest of turbulence, on the shoulders of the waves that envelop mind, energy, and matter, and that diffuse them into the atmosphere. (Conley, 1993, p. xv)

Stella Nona[1] is *a* geosurfing life. She takes pleasure in riding the world as on a wave. The wave constantly changes, is constantly moving, just like the world of a geosurfing life. Its constant folding, unfolding, and refolding intensities constitute an image of a world that moves in all directions at the same time, where there is no origin, no cause and effect and where everything is constantly in the making. Stella Nona is a hybridized child; a child who, for a moment at least, escapes a fixed definition. She is no longer the child with the attributes of naturalness and development[2]; she is a mixture of all that *and* the skilled, closer-to-his-twenties, wild-at-heart guy.

When we see Stella Nona's apprenticeship of walking from the perspective of a surfer's movements on the board, she produces, and is being produced as, movements of de- and reterritorialization.

The de- and reterritorializing movements are an important part of the philosophy put forward by the French philosophers Gilles Deleuze and Félix Guattari. They call this philosophy a 'geophilosophy', indicating a view of the world and our selves as being in constant transformation through movements of de- and reterritorialization. To deterritorialize implies to leave the territory that one presently inhabits. To reterritorialize means to form a new territory.

From this perspective we could as well understand Stella Nona's apprenticeship of walking in terms of a surfer's movements; the lying on the board with the hands well placed in the height of the armpits, the fast jump up with the feet close to the hands, into a squat position, the slight raising of the legs, the arms balancing horizontal to the body. This is an added image of the way a child learns to walk.

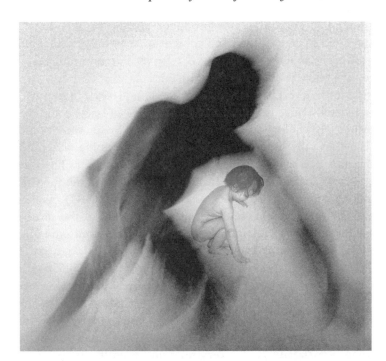

Figure 1: Surfer's movements superimposed on Stella Nona's novice steps (*Source*: Thor Jonsson)

It *does not give a new answer* to how a child correctly learns how to walk; it just opens up another way of appreciating a child's method of learning to walk. The new territory is never a return to the exact same conditions; something has changed. Stella Nona can be understood not as the child separated through specially defined characteristics from the adult, but as acting from another position, that of the surfer. The thinking that defines Stella Nona as a child separated by certain traits and characteristics is deterritorialized, and a new territory where it is possible to appreciate Stella Nona as a surfer is being created and reterritorialized. Stella Nona is deterritorialized from the naturally developing child to act in and reterritorialize a new territory as surfer. What we see is a territorializing movement of our thinking and understanding of the apprenticeship of walking of a young child.

The Territorialized Identity of the Pre-school Child

The notion of identity is normally thought of as something psychologically natural or socially constructed (Mozère, 2004). Consequently, the Swedish research group led by Professor Gunilla Dahlberg has found two dominating images of the identity of the pre-school child: the 'child as nature' and the 'child as reproducer of culture and knowledge' (Dahlberg, Moss & Pence, 1999; Dahlberg & Lenz Taguchi, 1994; Hultqvist, 1990; Lenz Taguchi, 2000; Nordin-Hultman, 2004). The child as nature is a child that has to be helped by adults to let free its *natural*, inherent capacities. This is to be done by activities such as free play (fri lek) and free creating (fritt skapande). The child as reproducer of culture and knowledge is a child who is supposed to receive the fixed content of knowledge presented by adults and to adapt itself to it, to internalize it, to *develop* in a certain manner, in order to later be able to reproduce it as exactly as possible.

According to Dahlberg & Lenz Taguchi (1994), these two images have their origin in the knowledge production realized by social science and, more specifically, developmental psychology. The theories of the Swiss developmental psychologist Jean Piaget and the American developmental psychologist Arnold Gesell have influenced Swedish pre-schools[3] since the Second World War. The naturally developing child is also an *individual* child. In Swedish pre-school the focus has been on each child's individual needs (Dahlberg & Lenz Taguchi, 1994). The two images, the natural and the reproducing child, coexist, are at work at the same time, and together with the focus on the individual child, they form a predominating notion of the identity of the learning pre-school child, as an individual, natural, developing child.

The apprenticeship of walking of the young child has, in this way, its written definition in the psycho-sociological theories surrounding early childhood education. Those involved in this practice, seeing a child who is in the process of learning to walk, see with eyes that are already coloured by the thinking of how such an apprenticeship is thought to function. It is a question of *recognizing* a child about whom we already know everything and then letting it stand as a *representation* that confirms what we already know. We see with eyes that are immersed in theories about a child's development. These theories are produced by the social sciences and more specifically theories from developmental psychology. They have taught us that a child develops in specific phases and patterns. A child who learns to walk has, for example, to first learn to crawl in a specific pattern. Developmental psychology, as it has been taught to and used by pre-school teachers, pre-supposes a natural child, a child with inherent capacities to develop the ability to walk according to a specific scheme. The pedagogical challenge lies in giving the right support at the right moment for the child to develop properly. The child's response to this developing help then indicates whether the child is following the normal curve of development or not. What the teacher is looking for is the *lack* of proper development; she/he is functioning as a detector of lack, an observer of *error* (Dahlberg & Lenz Taguchi, 1994).

Of course all this is being done with the best of intentions and good will. That a child develops seems unquestionably *true*, and to help the child develop properly seems unquestionably *right*. To see how the two dominating ideas of identity—as a natural or socially constructed feature—work in relation to the individual, natural, developing child, we turn now to the image of thought that Deleuze sees lying behind most attempts to think and act upon ourselves as subjects. According to Deleuze, most of the time we actually do not think at all: ' "Everybody" knows very well that in fact men think rarely, and more often under the impulse of a shock than in the excitement of a taste for thinking' (Deleuze, 1994, p. 132). To really think, for Deleuze, is a question of refusing what he calls an orthodox image of thought. This orthodox thought, the sort of thinking that we generally are busy exercising without too much trouble, involves representation and recognition. Thinking in this way reproduces that which we already see, understand or act upon in an endless circle of imitation. Within orthodox thought there can never be any true beginning or real difference, due to the hidden presuppositions behind thought. These presuppositions consist of the idea of thought as something natural and given. For example, when Descartes formulates *cogito ergo sum*, he claims to do away with all objective presuppositions, and to begin from a pure subject, but there are still subjective presuppositions. The I is never questioned as a natural feature; nor is what it means to think, nor to be (Deleuze, 1994, p. 129). Everybody is supposed to know what it means to be and to think.

This image of thought as a natural feature also embraces a direct relation with the true, passing through the 'common sense'. Since thinking is a natural feature and everybody knows what it means and exercises it without too much difficulty, such thinking is legitimized by our 'common sense'. This common sense is understood as 'a good will on the part of the thinker and an upright nature on the part of thought' (Deleuze, 1994, p. 131). Thought is amalgamated with truth and the good. Deleuze, then, calls this image of thought a dogmatic, orthodox, or moral image of thought, and it is, according to him and his findings in the writings of Nietzsche, only morality that can convince us of the good in thinker and thought and the amalgamated relation between thought and truth (Deleuze, 1994, p. 132).

In relation to the dominant identity of the pre-school child as an individual, natural, developing child, we can see how this dogmatic, orthodox or moral image of thought is working in defining the child as a natural and, by culture, defined individual. As a consequence of thought that is natural and true, the identity of the child is seen as a natural feature: the true child exists out there. As a consequence of thought that is connected to recognition and representation, the child needs to be recognized in its natural state and represented by the predetermined scale of proper development, defined by developmental psychology. Within the logic of measuring a child that is supposed to have inherent, natural capacities that need to be expressed according to a predetermined scale of development, the focus will be on each child. It becomes important to see where each individual is, in its natural state and then find out how this corresponds to the predetermined scale of development. The orthodox thought of recognition and representation functions in the way that the child is supposed to be out there somewhere, and needs to be discovered and *recognized* in it's individual, natural state, and compared and fitted into (or imitated in) the *representation* that developmental psychology has created as a map of a normal child.

The taken for granted connection between thought and common sense, as the good will of the thinker and the upright nature of thought, makes it almost impossible to contest that children individually and naturally develop. The moral character of these presuppositions makes it virtually incontestable that the recognizing and representing of the child is totally natural and true and in the best interest of each and every one. However, as several researchers have already shown,[4] the way developmental psychology has mapped the identity of the child implies a certain exclusion of children who do not fit the pattern of normal development. Theories of developmental psychology imply a normal curve of development for the child to follow. Developmental psychology defines a specific way to develop, through specific phases to reach a specific goal. A normal curve excludes all children who do not go through the predetermined development. They are not normal and become quite quickly objects of diverse psychological and pedagogical interventions so as to get the child on track. There seems to be something paradoxical about this individual child: how is it possible to talk about individuality, when there are only so many identities to take? If identity is supposed to be individual, but the child is still measured up against and corrected to fit an already determined scale of development, are we not, then, talking about a very limited kind of individuality? An individuality that really is nothing more than a convenient mechanism for organizing its subjects? Individuality as part of the pre-school child's identity, then, can be seen as nothing more than another drawn map of the desirable child for a pre-school practice. This becomes clear when we have to face children in pre-schools, who for one or another reason, do not fit into the stereotyped definition of individuality:

> Once you are in a pre-school or in a day-care centre each child's identity is limited to that of a preschooler or a day-care child. In other words the child's identity must conform to what is demanded. We all know that children who don't conform are problems in pre-schools or day-care centres. They bring in, or carry with them, aspects or fragments of identity that are unacceptable for the institution, which will then make use of different therapeutical, psychological or moral devices to try and get rid of what is then thought of as annoying, or even in some cases considered as deviant behaviours. (Mozère, 2004, p. 3)

Lately a new kind of image of the pre-school child has begun to emerge—that of the 'autonomous flexible child' (Dahlberg & Hultqvist, 2001). It is an image that at first glance seems to break with the codes of developmental psychology. The autonomous flexible child is a child who is independent, problem-solving and responsible for its own learning processes through self-reflection. This child is presumed to have a desire and ability to learn and is encouraged to ask questions, formulate problems and seek answers (ibid.). This image of the child could be seen as a challenge to the individual, natural developing child, since the ambition no longer is to map the child with the help of developmental psychology. But looking more closely, it seems that the focus on each individual is even more flagrant and outspoken in the image of the autonomous flexible child. Each child is supposed to have its own competencies to bring forward. These competencies are then being measured up to a new set of pre-determined goals and standards. Instead of being measured up to the scheme of development pre-established by developmental psychology, the child is now being measured up to grades of autonomous and flexible behaviour.

Lynn Fendler (2001) understands this new approach to the child as a matter of 'whole child education'; that is, it is no longer only the child's body or mind and moral behaviour that is supposed to be influenced by the pedagogic endeavours; now it is a question about getting at the child's very inner desires. It concerns an ambition to get children to want to learn and willingly adapt to the new logic of a continuous learning through problem solving.

> The thrust of 'whole child' education is that the child's entire being, desire, attitudes, wishes is caught up in the educative process. Educating the whole child means educating not only the cognitive, affective, and behavioural aspects, but also the child's innermost desires. There must be no residue of reluctance to learning; success for 'whole child' education means not only that the child learn, but the child desires to learn and is happy to learn. No aspect of the child must be left uneducated; education touches the spirit, soul, motivation, wishes, desires, dispositions, and attitudes of the child to be educated. (ibid., p. 205)

Fendler has shown that this child is far from being freer or less judged than the individual, natural, developing child. Nicolas Rose (1999) has demonstrated how this tendency towards autonomist and flexible behaviour is spreading into every corner of our society. We are finding ourselves under a new kind of governance, where the State no longer figures as a central governor, but each and every individual, through his/her reflected choices and seeking activity, designs her own life. It is not only the pupil in school who is supposed to be competent and researching with all the attributes described above. Everybody in today's society is supposed to take responsibility for his or her own life in a continuous process of learning (Fendler, 2001; Rose, 1999). It is from this logic that the term 'life-long learning' is born.

Deleuze predicted this new kind of governance in a text written in the late 1980s, where he describes this change as a movement from a disciplinary society into a control society, and where he shows how the term 'life long learning' is part of a new way of controlling people from the inside, so to speak, instead of, as earlier, disciplining them into desirable behaviours. According to him, we won't even need environments for shutting people in such as factories, prisons or schools. 'We are entering control societies that are being defined completely differently from disciplinary societies. Those who look after us no longer need, or will no longer need, environments for shutting people in' (Deleuze, 2004, p. 93, my translation). Instead, every individual is supposed to go through life in an endless process of continuous learning.

> One needs to pay careful attention to the subjects that are going to develop in 40 or 50 years and that says that the most fantastic thing would be to be able to go through school and working life at the same time. It would be interesting to know how the school and the working life, as part of a permanent education, would look. This is our future and it will no longer imply the accumulation of pupils in an environment for shutting people in. (ibid.)

By no means does Deleuze suggest that this is a future of freedom for the individual; it is just a question of a different kind of government, one of internal discipline instead of control coming from the outside affecting the individual.

> Control is not the same thing as discipline. With a highway you do not shut people in, but by constructing highways you increase the means of control. I am not saying that this is the only purpose of highways but

people can drive around as much as they want 'in freedom' without being shut in at all, at the same time as they are completely controlled. This is our future. (ibid.)

The competent, researching child, then, is still looked for in its natural state, but the natural state is now defined as a curious and knowledge-seeking individual, with a constant lust to learn. This time the measuring up, or the process of representing the child, is being done in relation to its degree of autonomous and flexible behaviour. The child need not only to be respons*ible*, but also 'respons*ready*' at any moment. And even though the characteristics of the desired outcome have changed, it is still a question of thought that is connected to the natural existing child and to progress. That the child 'out there' is natural and true seems then to be the case for both the notion of the individual, natural, developing child and the competent, researching child. This implies that despite the apparent changes in image there is still the same kind of orthodox thought at work behind the appearance. The child's identity as a natural and true feature still waits to be discovered. The model of recognition and representation is still very much alive.

Territorializing the Identity of the Pre-school Child—Indefinite Lines of Flight

What is important in the story of Stella Nona is to see how she is being defined as an individual, natural developing child in one context (the context of thought dominated by developmental psychology) and that she could also be defined as a surfer in another context (the context of thought that makes new associations and combinations). A young child learning how to walk could as well be understood as a surfer and the movements she/he goes through in surfing. This makes it possible to question the naturalness and truth of the descriptions of a learning child that we use. Imbedded in the thought of an individual, natural developing child is the idea that development necessarily goes in a specific direction. Development seems to indicate a movement forwards and upwards—a child learning more and more, better and better. The world seems to develop in a quantitative as well as qualitative way. Now, when we make an association like the one in the example of Stella Nona we disrupt this logic. It is possible to ask the question, 'and where do we really believe that we are heading?'. It is as if we all have a kind of silent agreement about pretending to know where we are heading, but is it not just a question about a kind of pretending? Do we all really know where our goal is? Are we not simply acting as if we believed that we know where we are heading? Deleuze (2004) talks about information and communication and how we are supposed to not just *believe in* communication and information pouring over us, but to *act as if* we believed.

Maybe walking is the function supporting the illusion that we are heading somewhere in life, but do we really walk ahead? Does everything develop for the better? What if we walk and walk and never get anywhere? When children walk, very often they do not walk with the purpose of getting ahead. So many things can happen on the way: you find something interesting on the sidewalk—a snail or a branch; or you find out that walking can be done backwards or in circles, or jumping on one leg. It seems as if the child's walking is more a question of exploring rhythm than of getting ahead.

Artist Monica Sand has been exploring walking in precisely this way, as a question of rhythm rather than as a movement forward. She uses a text from poet and songwriter Laurie Anderson to show how walking rather could be understood as a rhythm of falling and catching yourself.

> You're walking. And you don't always realize it,
> But you're always falling.
> With each step, you fall forward slightly.
> And then catch yourself from falling.
> Over and over, you're falling.
> And then catching yourself from falling.
> And this is how you can be walking and falling.
> At the same time. (Anderson, in Sand, 2005)

What Sand is challenging is not only the function of walking, but also the meaning of progress. She takes as a starting point the movement of walking, to trouble the entire idea of development in a movement forwards and upwards. She shows by referring to the story of Penelope and Odysseus how we believe that it is physical movement and change that indicates progress and production. Odysseus is the hero, travelling the seven seas performing heroic deeds, Penelope is just sitting around waiting for him, and the longer Odysseus stays away the more convinced everybody is that he will not be back. The suitors start to flock around Penelope and try to force her to make a choice among them for her new husband. Penelope then starts to weave; she promises her suitors that the day the weaving is completed she will make her choice. But since Penelope does not really fancy marrying any of the suitors she weaves during daytime and starts to undo the weaving during the night. At first sight, these actions appear to accomplish nothing: she does not get ahead; she produces nothing; she is still just waiting. But the way Sand reads it, Penelope is creating a rhythm that produces space and time for her. She does not do heroic deeds, she is not advancing, but she is producing. She is producing for herself time and space.

Sand uses these ideas of challenging progress and development in one of her installations. In a bridge in the town of Gothenburg on the west coast of Sweden she sets up a 40 metre high swing and lets a dancer swing there all hours of the day and night. When you swing, at the very moment the swing is at its highest point, turning to swing back again you are, for a short moment, weightless. Sand reads the movements of swinging as a rhythm very much like the rhythm of walking and weaving. Swinging is an activity that does not lead anywhere, you do not get ahead and you do not produce anything; and yet, from where does this extraordinary feeling come, that everyone who once has been on a swing remembers? Sand reads this feeling as a moment of liberation, a moment away from gravity that constantly pulls us back to earth. Gravity, according to her, can in this sense be translated to culture and the dominating ideas we have, for example, about identity. Our identity as child, adult, man, woman, white, black etc. is defined and we perform our actions according to the current definition of our identity; but from time to time we seem to find moments where these definitions no longer have a grip on us and we start producing something else. Swinging in this sense contains moments of being captured in gravity, culture or a specific definition of one's identity, but it also contains moments away from gravity, culture and already defined identities. These moments away from gravity or culture, though, are not connected to any progress or development as we normally think of it. It is not a question about being freer or more liberated, but about being liberated from whatever holds us back from making different experiences. It is, rather, a question about a kind of *freedom from*:

> If walking (here described as a fall without direction) is connected to earth you can in the swing (and in walking) have an experience of liberating yourself from that gravity that we in our culture name progress and development. What is being described is another kind of liberation, *liberation from progress and development.* In the same way as Penelope does, the swing creates a space—between the past and the future that is being widened by her own activity, (that might be called the present). '*The swing is going nowhere and neither are we*'. (Sand, 2005, p. 16)

This is very much what could be said is taking place in the de- and reterritorializing movements described in the story of Stella Nona. We live and act in one territory but from time to time we deterritorialize our current territory and start producing another one. We are stuck in patterns of behaviour and defined and specified as individuals: we live, sustain and continue to produce ourselves, as well as being produced as child, adult, woman, man, white, black, working class, upper class etc.; but now and then we produce a 'line of flight' (Deleuze & Guattari, 1994) out of our territory. There is no progress or development involved in a line of flight, it does not move forward or upward. Stella Nona does not learn how to walk in a better way as a surfer than as a child, she is just moving in another way. It is no longer useful to talk of good will in relation to how we treat a child surfer learning how to walk. It is not in Stella Nona's best interests for us to see her walking in line with the movements of a surfer on the board. Lines of flight are never pure; rather they are quite dirty. They bring with them fragments from the borders being crossed in the territorializing movements (Bonta & Protevi, 2004, p. 106).

There is something in the story of Stella Nona that seems familiar, and yet there is also something that offers us new experiences. Because there is no pre-determined image of the child as surfer, there is *no room for recognition and representation* in relation to a map of the child as surfer. Stella Nona learning how to walk as surfer is no longer solely defined by developmental psychology. This implies that she as a surfer *is not lacking* anything; she is just producing the same movements but in another way. It also implies that there is *no room for error* in the story: the invented dualism of true and false is abolished, in that the false does not have a shape of its own; rather, it is just giving shape to the true. *Truth cannot function* in the story of Stella Nona since there is no error to sustain its existence. The scheme of a young child's apprenticeship of walking is being disturbed. There are no longer predetermined phases on a predetermined development line. Rather there is a line that leads nowhere; it is simply a line away from being defined as a developing child in progress. 'Lines of flight can thus be seen as vectors of freedom, or at least freedom-from' (Bonta & Protevi, 2004, p. 107).

Notes

1. Stella Nona is my niece, at the time of the picture aged $1^{1}/_{2}$ years and just starting to walk.
2. These attributes are explained and critiqued at length in, for example, Dahlberg, Moss & Pence, 1999; Dahlberg & Lenz Taguchi, 1994; Hultqvist, 1990; Lenz Taguchi, 2000; and Nordin-Hultman, 2004.
3. In Sweden, children are welcomed in pre-school from the age of 1 year and they attend pre-school class at 6 years old and then primary school at 7 years old. The pre-school is considered to be the first step in the educational system and has its own curriculum, but there is a historically produced strong focus on the combination of care and education within the Swedish pre-school system. See further Dahlberg & Lenz Taguchi, 1994).
4. See, for example, Dahlberg, Moss & Pence, 1999; Dahlberg & Lenz Taguchi, 1994; Fendler 2001; Hultqvist, 1990; Lenz Taguchi, 2000; Nordin-Hultman, 2004; and Mozère, 2004.

References

Anderson, L. (1982/2005) Big Science Songs from United States I–IV, in: M. Sand (ed.), *Konsten att gunga Identitet som repetition och motstand pa en plats* (work in progress).

Bonta, M. & Protevi, J. (2004) *Deleuze and Geophilosophy: A guide and glossary* (Edinburgh, Edinburgh University Press).

Conley, T. (1993) Foreword, in: G. Deleuze, (1993) *The Fold: Leibniz and the Baroque*, T. Conley (trans. and foreword) (London, The Athlone Press).

Dahlberg, G. & Hultqvist, K. (eds) (2001) *Governing the Child in the New Millenium* (London, Routledge).

Dahlberg, G. & Lenz Taguchi, H. (1994) *Förskola och skola—om tva skilda traditioner och visionen om en mötesplats* (Stockholm, HLS Förlag).

Dahlberg, G., Moss, P. & Pence, A. (1999) *Beyond Quality in Early Childhood Education and Care: A postmodern perspective* (London, Falmer Press).

Deleuze, G. (1994) *Difference & Repetition* (London, The Athlone Press).

Deleuze, G. (2004) Qu'est-ce que c'est avoir une idée en cinéma, *Kairos*, 9:2.

Deleuze, G. & Guattari, F. (1994) *What is Philosophy?* (London, Verso).

Fendler, L. (2001) Educating Flexible Souls, in: G. Dahlberg & K. Hultqvist (eds), *Governing the Child in the New Millennium* (London, Routledge).

Hultqvist, K. (1990) *Förskolebarnet. En konstruktion för gemenskapen och den individuella frigörelsen* (Stockholm, Symposion).

Lenz Taguchi, H. (2000) *Emancipation och motstand dokumentation och kooperativa laroprocesser i forskolan* (Stockholm, HLS Forlag).

Mozère, L. (2004) What's the Trouble with Identity? Paper presented at the Reconceptualizing Early Childhood Education Conference in Oslo, Norway.

Nordin-Hultman, E. (2004) *Pedagogiska miljöer och barns subjektsskapande* (Stockholm, Liber Förlag).

Rose, N. (1999) *Powers of Freedom: Reframing political thought* (United Kingdom, Cambridge University Press).

Sand, M. (2005) *Konsten att gunga identitet som repetition och motstand pa en plats* (work in progress).

4

Deconstructing and Transgressing the Theory—Practice dichotomy in early childhood education

HILLEVI LENZ TAGUCHI
Institute of Education, Stockholm

Taking what is 'Already Happening' in Practice into Teacher Education

I first identified processes of deconstruction in a Swedish pre-school in 1997 (Lenz Taguchi, 2000).[3] The pre-school teachers tried to identify the dominant notions of children and learning, and transgress them by thinking and doing differently. They put central notions like 'the child' in a deconstructive process of *'sous rature'* (under erasure) (Derrida, 1976). To put the dominant meanings of 'the child' under erasure does not mean erasing, as in crossing out/over, deleting or throwing away. On the contrary, you cross out the first (or taken-for-granted) reading of the word, to be able to displace it (think it differently), but with the first meaning still remaining legible/readable (Spivak, 1976, p. xiv). In this way deconstruction means displacing meaning from '... wherever we are, in the text where we already believe ourselves to be' (Derrida, 1976, p. 162); i.e. the taken-for-granted and dominant meanings, in order to *re*construct something new, which is dependent on the old for its new displaced meanings. And these new meanings, in turn, need to be deconstructed, in a never ending process of what Derrida (1976) said entailed *'différance'*, traces, reversals, and displacements. Drawing from Derrida, feminist poststructuralism means actively practicing such a deconstructive process, in order for dominant meanings not to become normalizing and oppressive (Davies, 2000; Elam, 1994; Lather, 1991; Lenz Taguchi, 2000; 2004). Elam (1994) writes that feminism and deconstruction in alliance means being in a state of inexhaustible uncertainty and undecidability, while actively scrutinizing and resisting the normalizing effects of meanings. The word 'women', or, as in this case 'the child' or any pedagogical practice, becomes a 'permanently contested site of meaning' (Elam, 1994, p. 32). In other words, deconstruction, as a process of *re*doing by *un*doing, *re*formulating by *un*formulating, and *re*theorizing by *un*theorizing, is crucial to that which I will theorize as an ethic of 'resistance', affirmation and becoming.

In this article I make a point of trying to weave together the experiences of reconceptualized, poststructurally inspired early childhood practices (Canella, 1997; Canella & Grieshaber, 2001; Dahlberg, Moss & Pence, 1999; Dahlberg &

Moss, 2005; Davies, 2000; Lather, 2003; Lenz Taguchi, 2000; 2004; 2005a; 2006; MacNaughton, 2003; 2005), now going on throughout Sweden, with the experiences of the specific reconceptualized early childhood teacher education programs, made possible after the Teacher Education reform launched in 2001 (Bill, 1999/2000:135; Lenz Taguchi, 2005). I will mix examples from ECE practices with examples from teacher education, because these teacher education programs have actually taken *what is already happening* in practice into teacher education, and into a continuous dialogue, with students' vocational training as a basis.

I will start off with an excerpt from a project at a pre-school west of Stockholm (Åberg & Lenz Taguchi, 2005) that can, on the one hand, be understood as a metaphor for deconstructive and transgressing practices as such; but on the other hand, it is an example of what happened when the pre-school teachers managed to put strong dominant meanings of artistic work within early childhood education discourse, under erasure. The project started one day when a group of boys were climbing on top of each other as if they were performing a circus routine. The pre-school teacher asked what they were doing. 'We are making creations', a boy answered. The pre-school teacher Ann Åberg asked the four year old girl Alva:

— What is a creation?
— Look, Alva said, something becomes a creation when one builds with it. A pen is not a creation, but if you build with it becomes something else. It might become a creation.

The project grew into serious studies of sculpturing bodies and body-parts in clay, building and constructing in various materials. The children then became interested in using other media such as waste materials. The children called the items they collected gadgets. Viktor found something on the ground and asked:

— What is this gadget, do you think?
— I don't know, Ann Åberg said.
— Someone might know what this gadget is, but no one knows what it can become! said Viktor. (Åberg & Lenz Taguchi, 2005, p. 5)

The teacher's deconstructive approach meant letting go of taken-for-granted notions about children's artistic work, thus enabling the project to take unexpected turns. This project on 'creations' was *not* about doing artwork, as defined by the dominant discourse on the meaning of art in Swedish pre-schools, where children's creative work has been seen as expression of the child's inner psychological and cognitive development through essentialist and universal stages (Lind & Åsén, 1999). Instead this project involved studying bodies and objects in order to discover, not what they are, but what they might, under certain circumstances and in relation to other objects or body-parts, become! It was about an exploration of the becoming of things, and of welcoming and affirming the unknown (Derrida, 1976; 2003). This, states Derrida (2003), is what seems to be the hardest thing for us to do: welcoming the Other—what we don't already know. According to Derrida, to make something new is how deconstruction happens: through a process of not knowing, uncertainty, indeterminacy; being always a bit lost to one another. This is what makes possible a space for another kind of communication, learning and change (Lather, 2003). Or, as Chang has written on deconstruction as communication, such communication appears, 'when there is a moment, however minimal, of non-understanding, of *stupidity* with respect to what is said' (Chang, 1996, pp. 224–225).

Introducing Poststructural Theory and Its 'Linguistic Turn'

Poststructural theory, as in *after (post)* structuralism, took a decidedly linguistic turn away from the idea of uncovering essential and fundamentally unchangeable human traits as mental or societal structures, suggesting instead that nothing can be understood in any kind of way, without being given a meaning; i.e. without being *languaged* ('textualized').

As a fundamental critique of modernist epistemological theory of knowledge and learning, poststructuralism constitutes a move away from 20th century dominant constructivist learning theory, in education as in other social sciences. Instead of a separate subject making meaning of the object, as in constructivist theory, the subject–object dichotomy is dissolved and everything 'is' materialized meaning and meaning materialized. It becomes impossible to clearly separate what is the object in itself and what is our materialized, textualized meaning-making of it (Butler, 1997; 2004; Haraway, 1991). The meaning we give and make of things, actions, people and feelings, is collectively constituted and formulated within specific cultural and societal contexts; i.e. negotiated and renegotiated as a co-constructive process of meaning-making situated in time and place. Even the shapes and functions of the body have adapted to the meanings we have given them in specific (sub)cultures and contexts (Butler, 1993). The body is materialized by collectively negotiated, dominantly encompassed meanings, as is femininity, masculinity, sexuality, childhood and, for that matter, all forms of pedagogical practice. Consequently, those humans who we collectively consider as children, within a specific cultural and historical context, *'do' childhood*, by taking up (or occasionally resisting) dominantly accepted practices and ways of being a child specific to that historical and cultural context. This thinking illustrates a refusal to polarize and separate an 'unconditional and unchangeable nature', and our meaning-making/knowledge of it. Therefore, poststructuralism aims to dissolve some of the most fundamental western bipolar logics (Davies, 2000; Hekman, 1990; Lather, 1991; Lenz Taguchi, 2004). If theories in education, teaching and learning, and even we ourselves as learning subjects, are constituted by, and continuously reconstituted as collectively and culturally-specific materialized meaning-making; how, then, is it at all possible to know what is theory and what is practice? Where does theory end and practice begin, if practice is materialized meaning, and theory a set of meaning-making of lived life-practices?

The Modernist Theory-Practice Binary and the Beginning of Dissolution

Students come into teacher education thinking they will learn *what* truths to teach and *how* to teach them truthfully (Ellsworth, 1997). According to dominant notions there is a gap between theory and practice. It constitutes a binary, which is contaminated by the imagery of, on the one hand, a visionary, rational and logical, clean and flawless theory—an ideal state or condition; and on the other hand, a messy, dirty, unorderly practice, in need of being organized, cleaned up and saturated by the rationales and visions of theory.

In line with such imagery, theory is supposed to be applied to practice. But practice is *already* theoretical. In line with the poststructural thinking introduced above, the problem isn't that practice isn't doing what we think it theoretically could be doing, but rather that it is *already* doing educational theories, and much more than that. We are *already* speaking and performing theory into (this messy) existence of practice, along lines of thinking that are often contradictory, illogical and sometimes even counter-productive. Educational theories are *already* materializing, as developmentally appropriate, constructivist, response-ready, child-centred, adapted, open-minded, society-friendly, family and society focused practices; as layers and folds. We do this materializing as we talk and materialize *ourselves* as teachers/pedagogues into existence (Davies, 2000); as women or men, white, coloured, ethnic, religious, atheist, socially well- or less-well positioned, more or less intelligent, clever, emotional, practical, sensitive. We do this as we handle books, learning-material, furniture and school architecture, that are themselves already constituted by (i.e. materialized ideas of) knowledge, learning and the learning subject. Feminist philosopher Judith Butler illustrates the interdependence of theory and practice when she states that:

> [I]n all of these practices, theory is presupposed. We are all, in the very act of social transformation, lay philosophers, presupposing a vision of the world, of what is right, of what is just, of what is abhorrent, of what human action is and can be, of what constitutes the necessary and sufficient conditions of life. (Butler, 2004, p. 205)

As a consequence of such thinking when students enter our program I offer them an alternative imagery for the deconstructive processes in their education to come. I tell them that they did not come here with an empty toolbox needing to be filled with educational theories and methods, but rather with a toolbox *already filled* (and continuously refilling itself), with tools needing to be unpacked, investigated, and reformulated. Teacher education then will be about practicing a continuous process of unpacking and repacking what is already in this toolbox, relating it to other ways of thinking, and hopefully constructing new transgressive supplements. These, in turn, need to be deconstructed and reconsidered again and again, as a continuously self-reflexive process. It is by looking into, fumbling around in, and trying out the tools in this toolbox, that the inseparability and interdependence of theory and practice becomes obvious. And it is the 'order of things' (Foucault, 1998) within the toolbox, and the discursive power in the 'meaning(fullness)' of each tool, that gives this deceitful feeling of control, the willingness to subject oneself to truth-claims, but also, and importantly that simultaneous sense of being monitored and caught into a limiting closure (*clôture*) (Derrida, 1976). This activates in us a paradoxical desire to adhere to universalist truths and normality, while at the same time resisting those very same truths.

However, there is another central aspect of the theory-practice binary, a relation of power; where academic knowledge (that is predominantly theoretical and masculine), is more highly valued than (motherly feminine) pre-school-practices. This asymmetrical power-relation is discursively connected to other central modernist binaries, such as mind-body; thinking-acting/performing/experiencing; text-voice; seeing-listening; masculine-feminine, and ultimately, as are the sexed bodies that have performed science and pedagogical practice with children during the last century, men-women (compare the list of binaries in Davies, 2000, p. 51). Serious attempts have been made to upgrade practice and the value of vocational training during the last 20 years. But the theorization of what has been conceptualized as 'silent and experience-based knowledge' (Polanyi, 1983) to upgrade practice has basically failed. My understanding of such failure is that it stems from holding on to the dichotomy of theory-practice. The notion of practice is contaminated by the connotations of the unprivileged (feminine) side of the binaries listed above. This means holding on to modernist logocentric inclusionary or exclusionary thinking and thus a choice of *either-or*, instead of trying to make visible the interdependence and close connectedness between theory and practice that can blur the gap and even (momentarily) erase the binary.

Working towards blurring the gap between theory and practice, and making visible the interdependence requires, as I see it, deconstructively putting the central concepts and documented pedagogical practices under erasure (Derrida, 1976). This process makes practice visible as 'text'. In the very 'textualizing' of practice, it is, in fact, talked and written into existence—both as practice and as theory—and in that sense made accessible and even palpable, for being rewritten, re-talked, and thereby re-performed and transformed. Or, as Butler argues 'theory is itself transformative' (2004, p. 204).

The Teacher and the Student as a Learning Subjects

Drawing from Foucault, in opposition to a humanist unitary, coherent and essentialist Subject, feminist poststructuralism has theorized a discursively inscribed subjectivity, which is multiple, contradictory, and always in the making, continuously reinscribing itself (Butler, 1993; 1995; 1997; 2004; Davies, 2000). In line with such thinking the students need to encompass the *performative* character of language in the making of practice as well as individual subjectivity (Butler, 2004). Language, rather than representing the world, *effects* or *does* something; sets something in motion and transformation; materializes something. Gender, race and class can then be regarded, not as descriptive of identity, but rather as performative of identity (Fendler, 1999). Performative subjectivity then, is about how dominant discourses (social categorizations and meanings) constitute a power-production that performs *on/in(to)* the individual subject, who actively takes up such discourse and discursive practice, and materializes (for instance) white, middle-class, heterosexual femininity (Butler, 1993; 2004; Davies, 2000). In other words, student teachers need to understand how they *'do'* children of gender, race, ethnicity, disabilities, success and failure, as well as making themselves as teachers, while performing pedagogical practice and teaching 'innocent' contents of learning, that are already constitutive of the world and power production within that world. St. Pierre, writes about the relationship between experience, life and theory in terms of learning to conceive oneself in terms of the theory, because,

> ... living and theorizing produce each other; they structure each other. Not only do people produce theory, but *theory produces people* ... different theories of the subject make possible different lives. (St. Pierre, 2001, p. 142)

This is why teacher students' own memories or narrative writing of their experience as a child of early childhood education or schooling, or as a student at the Institute of Education, is an important aspect of these reconceptualizing teacher education practices. One of the ways that narratives are used is by examining them in relation to genealogical analyses of pre-schooling and different theories of learning (Burman, 1994; Lenz Taguchi, 2000; Nordin-Hultman, 2004; Walkerdine, 1998). This deconstructive work means identifying dominant, normalizing and resisting discourses and discursive practices in different and historically situated contexts, but also identifying paradigmatic shifts in discourses and practices in the history of early childhood education. Different theories of learning and knowledge, such as empiricism, instrumentalism, behaviourism, constructivism and social constructionism, as well as developmental and social psychology, view children, learning, and development differently. This has significant consequences for how learning-environments and learning-situations have been and are planned, organized and enacted. They also encompass inbuilt aspects of power-production. Viewing the child as a naturally growing plant, which the teacher can analyze the growth of, and recommend developmental help to, or simply leave alone; or viewing the child as an empty vessel needing to be filled up with knowledge or be trained, has different consequences in relation to power. Learning with the help of 'threat and/or carrots' is different from 'maturing from within', or being actively listened to or taken seriously in relation to how you as a child encompass and understand phenomena in the world around you. All theories, notions and expectations produce power, and thus construct the learning subject and learning differently, even those that we think are 'better' and more ethical than others (Lenz Taguchi, 2005a).

Unpacking Power Production in Teaching Practices

As students enter these programmes, after spending six months taking general courses at the Institute of Education, they are asked to write narratives that express their identity as, or current self-understanding of being or becoming, a student teacher; expressed in relation to an event and the feelings felt in the moment. The instructions are very simple. Students sit in small groups and formulate their narratives, and then write them down and read them to each other (compare Davies *et al.*, 2001). The narratives need not be 'true', but should express and make visible/tangible a central feeling or meaning/ 'experience'. Importantly experience here is not, as Joan Scott has claimed, 'the origin of our explanation, but that which we want to explain' (Scott, in St. Pierre, 2001, p. 142).

When the class meets again, some of the narratives are read out loud, and we start to 'read' from the perspectives of what meaning can be made, what dominant discourses of learning and teaching that are present, and what subject-positions are available for the subjects in the story, in relation to the academy, or in relation to other students and teachers. Also explored are shifts in such positionings, expressions of power and powerlessness, and feelings like joy or fright. To what extent are you positioning yourself, and to what extent are you positioned by others? Does gender matter? Does class or ethnicity matter? In many of the stories there is considerable ambivalence in relation to such questions. In some stories there is a definite repositioning of the subject, from a more insecure positioning about half a year earlier, as they first entered the Institute, to a position where it is possible for the student to materialize a subjectivity as a 'proper' student. Significant, however, is the discursive dominance of the teacher-educator's knowledge and practices that are to be taken up and accepted as models for understanding oneself as a student in a correct way. It is a process of being able to master certain practices, such as speaking openly and in a reflexive way in class, as in the story below.

> What if I didn't get in [to the Institute of Education]? Then everyone would know I couldn't do it. That I didn't belong there, since I wasn't the kind of person to study at the university. Only smart people do that. I didn't really believe I was a student until I actually sat there on the first day. It was so chaotic. But then I could feel how I grew from within, being able to come up with some good thinking now and then. And others would nod and agree. Eventually I could speak in a larger group, even without knowing exactly what to say, which is very much unlike me. I am becoming braver every day. I wonder why? Is it knowing more, or the being affirmed and encouraged? Sometimes I really can't believe I am a student at the university, and it happens that I step in front of the mirror and practice a little saying: I am a student. I am really a student!
> (Student 13 in Lenz Taguchi, 2005b)

The narrative above is written by a young woman, and reveals a position of insecurity that does not take for granted the possibility of 'really' becoming a student in the correct way. It can easily be read from a gender perspective where female students strive to do the right things to an extent that Davies *et al.* (2001) have shown even shapes and deforms the body just as much as the mind, and thus important aspects of subjectivity. The student needs to reconstruct her subjectivity using what she understands as dominant meanings of being a student correctly, by telling her mirrored image, as if 'writing on her body', that she 'really is' (materializes that specific correct and proper subjectivity as) a university student. The subject, states Butler, emerges both as the '*effect* of a prior power and as the *condition of possibility* for a radically conditioned form of agency' (Butler, 1997, pp. 14–15).

The narrative above, as the one below, is interesting in relation to the complexity of the concept of Foucaultian *subjectification* (Foucault, 1982; Butler, 1997), where the subject is simultaneously subjected, and subjects her-/himself (as an active 'agent'). Entering the university all students are subjected to an academic mastery discourse, entailing certain practices, theoretical conceptualizations, and an academic hierarchy to progress by fulfilling certain criteria, which are far from negotiable, and always dependent on a superior. The narratives can be read as the mastery discourse oppressing the students, as in being mastered by the academic discourse. On the other hand, as is sensed in the narrative above, the submission also entails a sometimes even joyous feeling of being able to master and mastery of that very same discourse. The process of subjectification takes place in such a paradoxical way, states Butler:

> ... submission and mastery take place simultaneously, and it is this paradoxical simultaneity that constitutes the ambivalence of subjection. ... the lived simultaneity of submission and mastery, and mastery as submission, is the condition of possibility for the subject itself. (Butler, 1995, pp. 45–46)

Walkerdine (1988) writes about this simultaneous process of being mastered and the joy of being able to master, which for many children, especially girls, of a lower social position in society, has had an effect of social mobility through education. In the story below, written by a young man, who positions himself very explicitly as working-class, it becomes evident that becoming a student is an extremely painful process, in the nexus of gender and social position. It illustrates a situation from an earlier course, revealing what can be read as male competitiveness in the obvious positioning of him as a student (early childhood teacher student) with a significantly less powerful position than the male teacher educator, towards whom his aggressive feelings are geared. He even reveals the same competitive and subjected position in relation to other (especially male) students in the group. Class and gender come together in this story as an aggressive resistance.

> Idiot! Is he enjoying himself now? How many concepts has he burped up that no regular human being has ever heard? Probably twenty-five—in ten minutes! He is probably very aware of this thinking: 'With a few difficult concepts I will be able to put down the new insecure students easily so they won't bother me. There are so many kids who apply for university who are not supposed to be in the academic world.' I bet that is just what he is thinking! Do the others really get what he is saying? They look interested enough anyway. That guy nods his head. Fake-ass! He probably doesn't understand more than I do. Hey! Can you explain what it is you are trying to say! Talk in a way that is understandable to me. Did I seriously miss out on so much in high school not to understand this? Am I the only one not understanding? Only me?! ... The social-democrats are part of this scheme. It is politically planned. They really don't want working-class kids to study. They want us to stay ignorant. That way they have secured their votes. That is why student's loans are impossible to live on, so that no one can afford to study anyway. ... What

is he saying now? How much have I missed out on? Damn. I better get out of here. But that is of course exactly what he wants! Of course it is. No, that would be too humiliating. Would he say something cocky if I did? Perhaps something sarcastic that I wouldn't even understand. Then he would exchange glances with some of the chosen few in the front row: 'There we got rid of another one of them!'. (Student 20 in Lenz Taguchi, 2005b)

The narrative can be read as the submissive aspect of the subjectification process, which, when reconstituting oneself as a student of the university, can be very difficult from a working class male point of view. The construction of masculinity in a predominantly female education, where students from different programs (early childhood education through upper secondary education) are mixed together in some courses, seems to be very difficult, with strong resistance and resentment as a result. Perhaps it is harder for men than women to submit to academic hierarchies and practices, simply because women already constitute their subjectivity in a subordinate position in relation to men. If this is (sometimes or often) so, do class, ethnicity and race matter? When and how does class, race or ethnicity make the construction of masculinity or femininity as a teacher or as an academic more difficult? And, to what extent is this relevant to how children in early childhood education construct their subjectivity as male or and female students in a relatively 'correct and proper' way? The questions that surfaced from our multiple readings of the narratives made the students aware of this ambivalent and simultaneously oppressive, resentful, and sometimes very empowering process of subjectification, on behalf both of themselves and the children they are about to teach.

Deconstructive Talks as an Ethic of 'Resistance', Affirmation and Becoming

I have elsewhere more thoroughly theorized the practice of deconstructive talks as a supplement to Habermasian (1985) communicative action (Lenz Taguchi, 2000; 2004; 2006). Habermasian theory of communicative action is, by itself, inadequate for the kind of negotiated learning practices important to postmodern education. Derrida's (1976) practice of writing '*sous rature*' (under erasure) works as a supplement to Habermasian theory in adding inclusionary, displacing and transgressing qualities to meaning-making as the central aspect of learning, and thereby transgressing the Habermasian aim of an agreed upon truth and the possibility of an intersubjective meaning-making and consensus in communication.

Deconstructive talk relies on difference (theorized from the Derridean concept of '*différance*') in the meaning-making process, rather than, as in Habermasian theory, on identifying 'truth', 'truthfulness' and 'rightness' in the communicated arguments (Habermas, 1985). In a deconstructive talk, difference is understood as a productive force rather than as a threat to consensus, or a problem to overcome (as in Habermasian theory). Deconstruction is about disruptions, destabilizations, undermining and challenging taken-for-granted notions, values, practices, and pedagogy 'as usual'. The major challenge in deconstructive talks is the requirement for self-reflection—thinking about *what and why* we see, hear, and value what we see, hear, and value. To exemplify, I briefly describe an example where a team of pre-school teachers and myself perform deconstructive talks during an investigational work with five year-olds in a project of orientating yourself in the environment of the pre-school, which can be followed in detail in another publication (Lenz Taguchi, 2006). Student teachers try out deconstructive talks in relation to the learning projects they perform with children during their repeated vocational training in the teacher education program.

The pre-school teachers in this example had asked the children to draw maps of who to change places with at the lunch table, after a request from the children to change places during lunch. The children made drawings ranging from the faces of those they wanted to change places with, to a variety of aerial maps. We were surprised by the variety of the drawings/maps, and decided to do multiple readings, by letting different theories of learning and ways of valuing the drawings make meaning. The multiple readings enabled us to resist what we previously took for granted to think differently about the drawings, and how we understood the work of the children. This made it possible to upgrade drawings that we in our first talk had given less value than others. As a consequence of the deconstructive talks we understood that there are multiple ways to understand children's drawings, and therefore multiple ways of valuing and encouraging children's thinking, drawing techniques, and co-operative understandings of what a map-drawing is or can be. But most of all, the deconstructive talks displaced our own taken-for-granted ways of understanding: firstly, what a map is or can be; and secondly, the impact on the map drawing session of such factors as: the teacher's questions and input in the drawing session with the children (as we viewed on the video-tape-document); the pre-conditions in terms of materials and the situatedness in time; as well as the relation to other assignments and activities going on at the pre-school. In other words, we didn't just learn about maps, but also about the importance of pedagogical preconditions and inputs, attitudes and teacher talk, and the effect on what children think, say and do. We had to actively 'resist' our own taken-for-granted ideas and notions about map-drawing, about children's competence, and about pedagogy/teaching, to be able to displace our readings and the way we thought about how to challenge the children in their learning the next day, and the next. Also, we were able to—ethically—identify multiple values of what the children did, the strategies they chose to use, often as a direct response to what the teachers had asked for, however unconsciously, as an attitude or taken-for-granted notion about maps or learning.

In other words, in a deconstructive talk the different readings are not valued as more or less true, as they would have been in a Habermasian communication, but are put side by side and treated equally important as different ways of understanding. If higher value is initially put on one reading, groups or individuals try to do a reversal, by forcing themselves to do an oppositional reading to which the higher value temporarily shifts. Additional readings serve as 'value equalizers,' and ideally make you displace all the readings in such a way that a state of 'both and' emerges. Such a 'both and' state is *not* about relativism, but rather about disrupting the normative and taken-for-granted, to ethically welcome readings and ways of understanding and doing that have been excluded or become invisible, or impossible to even think in the shadow of normative truth-claims. Resisting normative values and truths, displacing them and allowing, welcoming and affirming 'thinking-otherwise', encourages learning, challenges theorizing, thinking and doing in new ways. Furthermore it most often displaces power-production, and up-grades how we value the different competences of children. In this way deconstructive talks can enforce a strong ethical dimension, hence the conceptualization of an ethic of 'resistance', affirmation and becoming: '(It) explodes anew in every circumstance, demands a specific re-inscription, and hounds praxis unmercifully' (St. Pierre, 1997, p. 176).

No Objective 'Most Ethical' Choice: Just Openness to What 'May Be'

From both an individualistic and a broader social perspective, we choose a pedagogical method in order to 'do good.' Critics of a poststructurally-informed, deconstructive approach in ECE argue that it is too relativistic and too ambiguous. The critics argue that, by their very nature, eclectic practices are not sufficiently grounded in any one (universalist or better) theory and lack the normative qualities expected of a robust pedagogy. But, as the particularist ethical philosopher Ulrik Kihlbom argues, 'The morally competent or virtuous person is a moral ideal, which probably no one ever fully satisfies' (Kihlbom, 2002, p. 141). An ethical particularist stance, just as a poststructuralist stance, understands moral issues to be non-universalist, and that persons and actions must be understood contextually, the same way multiple readings of pedagogical practice are done contextually. We learn how to become morally competent persons within a specific social culture, although the existence of human virtuous ideals cannot be denied (Kihlbom, 2002). Derrida talks about the force of '*Necessity*', simultaneously acknowledging the necessity of human ideals and the necessity of questioning them (Derrida, 2003).

In another context Derrida clarifies his ethical thinking in relation to the process of deconstruction by making a difference between universal laws and rights ('*la droite*') and being ethically righteous ('*juste*'). The latter is a situated deconstruction of *la droite* in a radical openness to the specific Other, as part of a deconstructive ethic in education as a pedagogy of (what) 'may be' (Steinsholt, 2004).

A deconstructive ethic then, is about taking the wor(l)d very seriously in tracing and troubling signs of meaning, by way of absences and the otherness of what we think we know and believe. But it is also about the power of affirmation and welcoming what is beyond what we understand as present and possible. So deconstruction can never be about revealing new truths in a gesture of unmasking, revealing our ignorance and raising our consciousness to a higher level, as in a sublimation of 'having finally seen the light', or a Hegelian '*aufhebung*' into higher meaning (Spivak, 1976, p. xi). It is rather about holding on to an attitude of *indeterminacy and paradox*, as conditions of what Lather writes as 'affirmative power by undoing fixities and mapping new possibilities for playing out relations between identity and difference, margins and centres' (2003, p. 5). As teachers, all we can realistically hold ourselves accountable for is selecting the 'best' choice in relation to specific circumstances and specific children and ourselves as their teachers, on the basis of the deconstructive readings we have made (compare Lenz Taguchi, 2005a).

Transgressing the Theory-Practice Binary, Towards a New Professionalism as Pre-school Teacher

A new professionalism in pre-school teaching is about activating a certain kind of discursive 'resistance' necessary for identifying what and why we understand things the way we do: 'Any reading against the grain implies a detailed knowledge of the grain itself' (Davies, 2000, s. 114). The more you know about how the taken-for-granted notions in your own thinking have been constructed, the easier it is to resist such taken-for-granted thinking. Davies & Banks conclude:

> [I]ndividuals who understand the processes through which they are made subject are better positioned to resist particular forms of subjectivity, and thereby actively choose to think and do things differently. (Davies & Banks, 1995, p. 46)

This implies that the process of deconstruction can also make you reconsider your own subjectivity as teacher or student, and make it possible for you to resist thinking of yourself as a 'good and righteous' teacher, or as incompetent, or powerless, or authoritarian, as if that was a natural or inborn trait or fixed aspect of your subjectivity. In this sense deconstructive talks can, most often, have strong emancipatory effects on its participants. Not having to always think that there must be one truth about children's learning, or one right way of doing something with the children, has proven to be very emancipating, both to teachers as well as to student teachers (Lenz Taguchi, 2000; 2005a; 2006).

Using various deconstructive practices in the context of teacher education is about seeking 'that intersection of material transformation through theory's practice and practice's theory' (Lather, 2003, p. 7). Being a professional teacher or researcher is about acknowledging—down into the bare bone—how theory and practice are interdependent, and in a certain understanding, one and the same (Lenz Taguchi, 2004). So, as we perform pedagogical practices, we (unconsciously) theorize them into existence, and with an awareness of this, we start to reflect upon practice theoretically, and trouble our own understandings. This way, deconstructive processes become part of our professionalism, as we think deeply and critically about how we stage, arrange, do and analyze our pedagogical performances. We do multiple readings, or repeated analysis, to understand the same situation in many ways. This helps us to make situated ethical choices about what we will do next to challenge the children and students to be curiously engaged in their learning processes. The deconstructive process can thus be understood as a simultaneous move of tracing and troubling meaning, and an ethical affirmation of renegotiated meanings and values.

An Affirmation Of the 'Wholly Other' as a New Becoming

A (deconstructive) methodology, must be 'out of practice', to be, I dare to say, 'in(to) practice'. It accounts for a response to 'the call of the wholly Other' (Lather, 2003, p. 5). This is what constitutes what Lather has called an 'ethical turn' in the human and social sciences. Such ethic is about welcoming, and an affirmation of the Other; of your fellow colleagues; of the children you teach/learn with, and their families (Dahlberg & Moss, 2005; Lenz Taguchi, 2004; 2006). Without the Other, no meaning at all can be constructed, and no deconstruction can be made. No practice constitutes itself without a meaning-bearing witness in the Other, and no re-constituting of practice can be made without the *différance* made visible in the Other, or at least in the always non identical repetition of your own practice that can also be understood as Other. The Other, whether it is the Otherness of your own always reformulated thinking or reconstituted performative practice, or the Other as in the Other human being; i.e. the child, your colleague or the family, is the precondition for the pre-school practice as such. Without the Other there is no idea or practice of a pre-school; no child; no family; no pre-school teacher. Deconstructive practices make us aware of the necessity of the Other in a process of 'becoming ourselves'; as subjects.

A deconstructive ethic is incomprehensible without the recognition and affirmation of the Other, and equally important, this is what makes it at all desirable. This is important, because we need to ask ourselves why it is at all desirable for student teachers as well as pre-school teachers to engage in practices of deconstruction; i.e. to perform seemingly endless documentation of practices and learning-processes, and engage in long and demanding deconstructive talks and thinking. To answer this and to conclude this article, I want to turn to Hegel's Phenomenology of Spirit, where he states that desire:

> '... is essential to self-reflection, and there is no self-reflection except through the drama of reciprocal recognition. Thus the desire for recognition is the one in which desire seeks its reflection in the Other. This is at once a desire that seeks to negate the alterity of the Other (it is, after all, by virtue of its structural similarity to me, in my place, threatening my unitary existence) and a desire that finds itself in the bind of requiring that very Other whom one fears to be and to be captured by; indeed, without this constituting passionate bind, there can be no recognition. One's consciousness finds that it is lost, lost in the Other, that it has come outside itself, that it finds itself as the other or, indeed *in* the Other. Thus recognition begins with the insight that one is lost in the Other, appropriated in and by an alterity that is and is not oneself'. (cited in Butler, 2004, p. 240)

Recognition and affirmation of the Other is what makes us speaking and knowing, and co-operatively meaning-making human beings. Renegotiating, reformulating, repracticing that meaning-making is what living is all about, and therefore also what, at the end of the day, pre-schooling and pre-school teaching is all about. An ethic of 'resistance', affirmation and becoming starts with questioning and deconstructing the taken for granted split and dichotomy of theory-practice, by performing deconstructive processes on your every day practice; not to correct it towards a visionary or universally good end state, but, to facilitate a process of becoming. Recalling 5 year-old Viktor's words about the creation-project, I say: Someone might know what a pre-school teacher, pre-school, pedagogy or teaching is, but no one knows what it might become!

Notes

1. ECE practices in Sweden have been regulated by the Social Ministry and the Board of Social Affairs up until 1996, when ECE was integrated into the school system. The first state curriculum for ECE practices was legislated in 1998. ECE is now the first part of a life long learning system in Sweden regulated by the Educational Ministry. In the Swedish system there is only one integrated institution for care, health and education of children, encompassing the ages 0–5 years. This integrated form of school/care is formally called pre-school, and gives all 1 year olds and older children the right to a full-day service, irrespective of whether the parents work or study, or whether they are on parental leave or unemployed. Six year olds can attend pre-school class on school premises, or stay in pre-school. The school starting age in Sweden is 7 years, but 98% of all the 6 year-olds are enrolled in pre-school class. (For further information on this see Lenz Taguchi & Munkhammar, 2003.)
2. These programs are $1-1^1/_2$ years long and enrol about 75 students per year. They are aimed at teaching children from the age of 0 to 10, in pre-schools and schools. One program is called 'Investigative pedagogy' and the other 'Children and natural sciences.' Both programs use pedagogical documentation and aesthetic learning-processes involving many different media in courses such as 'Investigative mathematics, with dance/bodily movement, music and drawing' (See Lenz Taguchi, 2000; 2005).
3. During the last 15 years the Swedish Reggio Emilia institute, as well as the research team at the Institute of Education in Stockholm under the supervision of Professor Gunilla Dahlberg, has encouraged, enforced and studied practices of investigative and co-operative learning processes amongst children in different municipalities around Sweden. Some of these pre-schools have turned out to perform cutting edge work seriously challenging the *theory-practice* dichotomy, using post-structural and feminist theory/ practice with(in) a deconstructive move/shift (Dahlberg, Moss & Pence, 1999; Åberg & Lenz Taguchi, 2005).

References

Åberg, A. & Lenz Taguchi, H. (2005) *Lyssnandets pedagogik. Demokrati och etik iförskolans lärande* [Pedagogy of listening. Democracy and ethics in pre-school learning practice] (Stockholm, Liber).

Bill 1999/2000:135. *En förnyad lärarutbildning* [A renewed teacher-education] (Stockholm, Ministry of Education).

Burman, E. (1994) *Deconstructing Developmental Psychology* (New York/London, Routledge).

Butler, J. (1993) *Bodies That Matter: On the discursive limits of 'sex'* (New York/London, Routledge).

Butler, J. (1995) For a Careful Reading, in: S. Benhabib, J. Butler, D. Cornell & N. Fraser (eds), *Feminist Contentions: A philosophical exchange* (New York, Routledge).

Butler, J. (1997) *The Psychic Life of Power: Theories in subjection* (Stanford, CA, Stanford University Press).

Butler, J. (2004) *Undoing Gender* (New York/London, Routledge).

Canella, G. (1997) *Deconstructing Early Childhood Education. Social justice & revolution* (New York, Peter Lang).

Canella, G & Grieshaber, S. (2001) *Embracing Identities in Early Childhood Education. Diversity and possibilities* (New York, Teachers College Press, Columbia University).

Chang, B. G. (1996) *Deconstructing Communication, Representation, Subject, and Economies of Exchange* (Minneapolis, University of Minnesota Press).

Dahlberg, G. Moss, P. & Pence, A. (1999) *Beyond Quality in Early Childhood Education and Care. A postmodern perspective* (London, Falmer Press).

Dahlberg, G. & Moss, P. (2005) *Ethics and Politics in Early Childhood Education.* (Oxford/New York, Routledge/Falmer).

Davies, B. (2000) *A Body of Writing 1990–1999* (Walnut Creek, CA, AltaMira Press).

Davies, B. & Banks, C. (1995) The Gender Trap: A feminist poststructuralist analysis of primary school children's talk about gender, in: J. Holland & M. Blair (eds), *Debates and Issues in Feminist Research and Pedagogy: A Reader* (London, The Open University).

Davies, B., Dormer, S., Gannon, S., Lenz Taguchi, H., Laws, C., McCann, H. & Rocco, S. (2001) Becoming School-girls: The ambivalent project of subjectification, *Gender and Education*, 3:2, pp. 167–182.

Derrida, J. (1976) *Of Grammatology* (Baltimore, MD, The John Hopkins University Press).

Derrida, J. (2003) Following Theory, in: M. Payne & J. Schad (eds), *Life After Theory* (London/New York, Continuum).

Elam, D. (1994) *Feminism and Deconstruction. Ms. En Abyme* (London/New York, Routledge).

Ellsworth, E. (1997) *Teaching Positions: Difference, pedagogy, and the power of address* (New York, Teachers College Press, Columbia University).

Fendler, L. (1999) *Making Trouble: Predictability, agency, and critical intellectuals: 'All reification is a forgetting'* in: L. Lundahl & T. Popkewitz (eds), *Education, Research, and Society. Critical Perspectives from American and Swedish Graduate Students* (Umeå University, Monographs on Teacher Education and Research, vol. 3).

Foucault, M. (1982) The Subject and Power, in: H. L. Dreyfus & P. Rabinow (eds), *Michel Foucault. Beyond structuralism and hermeneutic* (Hertfordshire, The Harvester Press).

Foucault, M. (1998) *Aesthetics: The essential works, vol. 2,* J. Faubion ed., Harmondsworth, The Penguin Press).

Habermas, J. (1985) *The Theory of Communicative Action, Volume 1: Reason and the rationalization of Society* (Boston, Beacon Press).

Haraway, D. (1991) *Simians, Cyborgs, and Women. The reinvention of nature* (New York, Routledge).

Hekman, S. (1990) *Gender and Knowledge. Elements of postmodern feminism* (Cambridge/Oxford, Polity Press).

Kihlbom, U. (2002) *Ethical Particularism. An essay on moral reason* (ACTA Universtatis Miensis. Stockholm Studies in Philosohpy 23, Almqvist & Wiksell International).

Lather, P. (1991) *Getting Smart: Feminist research and pedagogy with/in the postmodern* (New York/London, Routledge).

Lather, P. (2003) Applied Derrida: (Mis)reading the work of mourning in educational research, philosophy and education, *Educational Philosophy and Theory*, 35:3, pp. 257–270.

Lenz Taguchi, H. (2000) *Emancipation och motstånd. Dokumentation och kooperativa läroprocesser i förskolan* [Emancipation and Resistance. Documentation and co-operative learning-processes]. PhD dissertation. (Stockholm, HLS Förlag).

Lenz Taguchi, H. (2004) *In på bara benet. En introduktion till feministisk poststructuralism* [Down into bare bone. An introduction to feminist poststructuralism] (Stockholm, HLS Förlag).

Lenz Taguchi, H. (2005) Developing an Integrated Workforce: The new teacher education in Sweden, *Children in Scotland*, November.

Lenz Taguchi, H. (2005a) Getting Personal: how early childhood teacher education troubles students' and teacher educators' identities regarding subjectivity and feminism *Contemporary Issues in Early Childhood Education*, 6:3, pp. 244–255.

Lenz Taguchi, H. (2005b) Transcribed tape-recorded documentation from the research project.

Lenz Taguchi, H. (2006) Reconceptualizing Early Childhood Education: Challenging taken-for-granted ideas, in: J. Einarsdóttir & J. T. Wagner, *Nordic Perspectives in Early Childhood Education* (Charlotte, NC, Information Age Publishing).

Lenz Taguchi, H. & Munkhammar, I. (2003) *Consolidating Governmental Early Childhood Education and Care Services under the Ministry of Education and Science: A Swedish case study* (Early Childhood and Family Policy Series, No 6—2003: UNESCO Education Sector).

Lind, U. & Åsén, G. (1999) *En annan skola—elevers bilder av skolan som kunskapsrum och social arena* [Another school—students images of school as a space of knowledge and a social arena] (Stockholm, HLS Förlag).

MacNaughton, G. (2003) Shaping Early Childhood. Learners, curriculum and context (Glasgow, Open University Press).

MacNaughton, G. (2005) *Doing Foucault in Early Childhood Studies* (London/New York, Routledge/Falmer).

Nordin-Hultman, E. (2004) *Pedagogiska miljöer och barns subjektsskapande* [Pedagogical Environment and the Construction of Children's Subjectivity] (Stockholm, Liber).

Polanyi, M. (1983) *The Tacit Dimension* (Gloucester, MA, Peter Smith).

Spivak, G. C. (1976) Translator's Preface. In J. Derrida, *Of Grammatology* (Baltimore, MD, The Johns Hopkins University Press).

Steinsholt, K. (2004) *Steinsholt Live* (Trondheim, Tapir Akademisk Forlag).

St. Pierre, E. A. (1997) Methodology in the Fold and the Irruption of Transgressive Data, *Qualitative Studies in Education*, 10:2, pp. 175–189.

St. Pierre, E. A. (2001) Coming to Theory: Finding Foucault and Deleuze, in: K. Weiler (ed.) *Feminist Engagements. Reading, resisting, and revisioning male theorists in education and cultural studies* (New York/London, Routledge).

Walkerdine, V. (1988) *The Mastery of Reason: Cognitive development and the production of rationality* (London, Routledge).

Walkerdine, V. (1998) *Counting Girls Out: Girls and mathematics* (London, Falmer).

5

In Early Childhood: What's language about?

LIANE MOZÈRE

This chapter makes use of Foucault's work, along with Deleuze and Guattari's conceptualizations;[1] to step away from the usual psychological Piagetian paradigms in Early Childhood, where children are supposed to conform to predictable developmental stages, or to universal patterns such as the Freudian Oedipus complex. Having been involved in research for over thirty-five years with gender issues in Early Childhood, I have been able to show and analyze how childhood, considered by Ariès as a modern 'invention', has been closely linked to the diminished status of the women caring for children. In other words, we see an ever-progressing analysis of childhood as an imperfection, as a lack which society has to 'fill' during the socialization process, thus transforming young children, in ancient times animal-like or devilish beings (i.e. the incomplete and imperfect *infans*), into acceptable adults (through magic rituals or baptism for example). Adulthood is thus understood as a fulfilment for childhood. This lower status childhood is in a way coherent with the inferiorization of the women seen as 'naturally' able to care for young children (Mozère, 1977, 1992, 2004).

This research was conducted in French daycare centres, where staff are faced with an impossible role, insofar as the idealized mother-child relationship is seen as the only acceptable model of appropriate care for children under the age of three. In France, children attend *école maternelle* (nursery schools which are mainly education oriented) until age six, when compulsory schooling begins. Daycare in such a view is only a stopgap and it is seen as impossible for the staff to offer appropriate care to the young children. Their role in the past was mainly ancillary revolving around matters of hygiene, but now that some psychological and psychoanalytical inputs have been incorporated, our latest research shows that these women in daycare develop immense, unvalued, unrecognized and invisible competencies, not only with the young children they care for, but with adults (other members of the staff and parents) where they need to make use of capacities they were never taught. So, in a way, the two major actors/actresses in the play—the young children and the staff (all female)—assume minor roles. That is the reason I suggest a mind shift in order to analyze things in another way. In order to do this it is necessary to present a brief sketch of the model I would like to move away from.

So-called 'normal' development is traced to standardized stages of development through which every singular child is 'supposed' to pass in order to become a 'normal' adult. These standards are, one must never forget, merely statistical averages that rely on analysis of cohorts that are supposedly homogeneous and stable. A child is supposed to walk at age one and to talk at age two. But everyone is aware that each single, unique child follows its own paths to become a unique and singular adult, an adult that is not a homogeneous addition of standard qualities or competencies, but an agency. As Rimbaud put it 'I is another'. In other words, it is less about an 'or/or' arrangement than a 'and/and' process. In Foucault's (1976) societies of discipline, each singularity (or person) is supposed to conform to fixed behaviours and attitudes that enable society to function. In most usual perceptions *pathos* is a deviation from the norm. On the contrary, Georges Canguilhem, a French philosopher and medical doctor who had an important influence on Foucault's work, analyzes *pathos* as the phenomenon that creates *logos* (1985). It is when you have fever, a sore back, or a headache, that you notice that something is *not* normal. For Canguilhem the norm is only a state of innocence of the organism that is necessarily betrayed. Norms are not there first; it is *pathos* that creates the need to define norms. This shift is central for whoever wishes to understand what the nature of the illusion in the 'progressive', stage-defined, developmental analysis actually deals with. In the same way Foucault writes that one can only apply the law on leaning on and making use of illegalisms in accounting for and as elements of the picture (*Dits et Ecrits*, 1994).

So, turning back to the 'normal' child, she/he is first defined as an adult to be, lacking inches, dexterity, capabilities and competencies, all of which will be attained if she/he develops properly according to the prevailing standards in a given society. The typically Hegelian negativity of such a point of view leads one to consider *lack* as necessary to be completed by acquiring something 'more' (inches, weight, etc), which will then help the child to grow more mature, more adult; as if life were just a continuum of fixed and predictable stages, the same for all. But such a vision is, thanks to Foucault's conceptualizations, very impoverishing and doesn't contribute to an understanding of what is at stake in early childhood, or even in so called adulthood.

When Foucault talks about societies of discipline he speaks about a *coup de force*, in the words of Nietzsche, which changes the prevailing status quo. For example, in the 17th century when the *dispositif* of power/knowledge of modern Psychiatry creates the phenomenon of the *Grand Renfermement* separating the insane from other outsiders of the society (the poor, the mad people, the beggars, and the sick); it labels the mad as insane, enabling psychiatrists to ground their power and knowledge position. This *coup de force* creates a new social (or sociological) category— the 'insane', who will be submitted or subjected to the now prevailing norms in terms of the opposition, 'sane/insane'.

In the field of Early Childhood, philanthropic organisations created *crèches* in order to separate specific poor infants from other infants dwelling in slums and living amongst immoral, barbarous and unmarried workers. Those who were thus 'chosen', enabling a good deed to be fulfilled by the paternalistic philanthropists, would get access to these *crèches* when their parents were trustworthy, married in Church, sober and submissive. This process gives birth to the 'normal' crèche child, which can then be saved from the evils of moral corruption and promiscuity that is, in the minds of the philanthropists, never very far from revolutionary dangers. Before the major discoveries of asepsis, the fate of these children was not enviable since severe rates of infant mortality developed in these crèches (Mozère, 1977, 1992). The hygienic period that follows also patterns a standardized 'normal' child in terms of physical health norms that will gradually overcome the damages of infant mortality. This 'biopower', as Foucault calls it, imposing radical campaigns against contagion and morbidity, would of course lead to improved national health standards, but was always grounded on the idea of normality which would in time be used by developmental psychology and, later psychoanalysis.

What this brief evolution story does is to shed light on the naturalization of the so-called norms that hide and occult (overshadow) the multiplicities that live in each small child as a pure singularity. Turning back to Canguilhem's (1985) argument, it is when something goes wrong—when the baby grows too 'slowly', when it doesn't achieve a normal weight or is not interested in occupations of it's age—that knowledge/power (*dispositif*) is brought to attention, resulting in orders, injunctions and protocols that are supposed to bring back order where disorder has been detected. Contrary to an ethno-methodological conceptualization, disorder must be eradicated instead of being analyzed as another form of order (Garfinkel, 1996). This same form of patterning has been the case for centuries—in our civilization as well as in others. Babies are massaged, their bodies shaped, decorated, tattooed and scarred in so-called primitive societies. In pre-revolutionary France, the skull was shaped, the ears and body tightly bandaged, in order to save the new born from animality and evil. Walking was also kept under strict control, thanks to clothing that would hold the child upright so that it would not return to the state of a crawling creature (Mozère, 2006a, 2006b).

Of course this idea of the normalized child is utopian; children escape the yoke, they flee the models and freely make use of all opportunities that may occur. Their serendipity is like our own; each time we act and behave, not in terms of observance of rules and norms, but following the 'lines of flight' of desire (Deleuze & Guattari, 1980). It is this path I would like to follow in this chapter, very much a work in progress with plenty yet to be done. For a long time, pedagogues have realised that a child needs not to conform, but to be accompanied by benevolent peers or/and adults. Comenius is well known to have created a small school of the Maternal Bosom. Later Fröbel invented kindergartens (children's gardens) where they could develop according to their own tempo and desire (Mozère, 1998).

Although Lawrence Hirschfeld (2002) wonders why anthropologists don't like children, his enlightening article gives an example of how children are not only an addition of lacking characteristics, but have potential and are creators. He first shows the way children develop 'semi-autonomous subcultures' and manage to participate in highly specialized activities in the absence of adults, as they also develop and sustain social practices, networks of relations and specific codes. Although this is usually observed when children are, on average, aged five or six, Hirschman shows with the example of a game 'the cooties' that younger children (age two upwards) are also able to show such competences. This game children created is based on a sort of a disease that contaminates you invisibly but nevertheless takes place in a social setting: you catch cooties, you try to get rid of them in passing them to another child (eventually of another group) and you develop all sorts of prophylactic tricks to keep them away, by catching them in paper traps, simulating having been bitten, crossing your fingers in a certain way, climbing on a pole, locking the doors or switching off the lights. So cooties are invisible, but the practical actions they create are observable and what is most striking is that someone may have cooties and later on have none. What *is* sure about cooties is that their action is unpredictable. The ability of even very young children to deal with an invisible contamination of an 'abstract substance' is highly demonstrative of the fact that young children are pure potentialities.

Other researchers such as Julie Delalande (2003) have shown how preschoolers 'play smooth sand', developing a whole ritual. The same is the case in a Swedish Daghem (daycare centre) where children at age two built a 'creation' with their bodies startling the supervisor, or playing with their shadows using a projector and inventing rituals the adults misinterpreted in terms of fear (the children were yelling, 'ghost, ghost'. But it turned out they were just using the *sound* 'ghost' to give another turn to the game, which had nothing to do with fear (Borgnon, 2005). These children are far from being what Deleuze and Guattari call the 'dried-up' child that has to hide and repress its desires in order to fulfil what is demanded of him (1980). Some young children never un-conform, some manage to build some backstage strategies such as Erving Goffman (1968) analyzes in *Asylum*. But those children have to stick to the identity that is given them through the *coup de force* we talked about above.

In the French compulsory school system, it is expected that a child of six will master reading after eight months schooling; otherwise there's a problem. Children considered in terms of normative stereotypes are always a problem of some kind: it's another way of considering children as eternally lacking beings. Identity is patterned by these successive *coups de force* that turn a normal infant into a normal toddler, a normal preschooler, and so on. On the other hand, the examples given above show how unexpected, or even unthinkable or impossible encounters provide opportunities for creation and forms of life opposed to stereotypes and norms.

For the two last years I have been involved in empirical research with staff of daycare centres in France (crèches). There, staff are trained for one year and usually stay in the same crèche for the long term, with practically no possibility of promotion. They are subjected to constant—and constantly changing—recommendations from medical doctors or psychologists. Crèches are centres that welcome children from four months to three years old. They have one staff member for every five babies and one adult for every eight walking children. Once French children reach the age of three, they are all in pre-school *écoles maternelles*, which are 'real' schools with one teacher for 20 or more children in a single classroom. While *crèches* are funded by public money, parents are required to pay fees; whereas *écoles maternelles* are free of charge for the parents. I will focus here only on *crèches* where my research was conducted during four years in a Northern suburb of Paris.

About sixty staff members were interviewed in groups, with interviews and group discussions organized six times a year. This research enabled me to show how a new form of normalization has developed recently in daycare centres, reinforcing the (till then) prevailing norms. In a certain number of crèches, staff are not supposed to kiss or to hug the children because the latter might become confused (taking them for their mothers!). A baby or a child should never sit in the lap of a staff member because there is a danger of sexual contact with the adult. If a child touches the body of a staff member, she must always tell the child 'this is my body'. A baby should not be cradled because it can be interpreted as masturbation, and, last but not least, one shouldn't take the temperature via the rectum because it is considered a form of rape. It is obvious that all these injunctions, these orders, have concrete and material consequences on the way to handle children and their bodies, but there are also impacts on the way adults interact with them. In other words, what space is there left for the child's desire; i.e. its singular language that is verbal, non-verbal, corporeal, sensitive, perceptive?

This language of desire I've been dealing with in such a pattern of normalization is always untimely, misplaced; it's always rowdy, unexpected. And that 'disorder' is exactly what the idea of identity (Mozère, 2006a) and the new protocols tend to subject and to annihilate. But now this research makes it possible to show the way these workers enabled children to access the language of desire, just by staying aware of the creations of the children, by being open to their experimenting paths, discoveries, and shortcuts. The stories I'm going to tell are, in a way, experiences everyone may have had with children, but what I want to stress here is the following. What I called these great unrecognized inventions the staff in the crèches enabled the children to experience are practical arrangements, where each time some of what is supposed to be their identity or the normal way of seeing things is revisited, is questioned, and so the normalization system is partly forced to give way to emancipatory forces of desire.

In other words, it's not the examples that are interesting *per se*; it is the way they are considered, the different standpoint that is adopted, that I see as important. This requires a mind shift that makes it possible to 'hear' these whispering languages, to 'notice' these tiny micro-events that make the lines move, that blur the conventional picture. It is a way to bypass the cognitivist control that tends to educate and conform young children in order to maintain the *status quo*. It is a way to make use of their desire to learn, to channel it through codes that enable it to be castrated of its potential subversion that is at the core of desire (Mozère, 2006a, 2006b). Two vignettes can illustrate this.

> Sophie arrives this morning and tells Annie (the staff member), 'I have a kitten in my hand.' 'Oh,' says Annie, 'may I have a look?' and they pretend to look at the kitten. Sophie is busy playing around and suddenly Annie asks her whether she wouldn't like her to keep the kitten while she plays. Sophie accepts and Annie looks after the kitten. After lunchtime and before the nap, Sophie asks Annie to give back the kitten.

Another vignette:

> One morning Dany asks the children, because it's a nice sunny day, 'Why couldn't we go to the beach?' So the children telephone their parents to

ask them for permission, and to bring their bathing suits, towels and sun cream. All the parents bring what is needed, Dany and the children take the tube to the station and take the train to the beach. There they undress, put on their bathing suits, put on sun cream and rush into the water. Suddenly Dany hears Charlotte shriek, 'Oh you splashed me'.

This language could be thought of as mere examples of imagination or fantasies, but I posit it has to do with the most vivid manifestations about what desire is for these children, and I would like to illustrate this by presenting the work of a French social worker I would call a magician-therapist, i.e. non conformist and creative. Fernand Deligny, who first dealt with delinquent boys after World War II, had created a very special way of handling them. Instead of keeping the boys in specialized centres, he organized trips through the countryside and in the mountains, sharing their daily life and camping. This adventure he called La Grande Cordée (the Big Roped party). Much later, he created a 'suitable place to live in' (which in French was called after 1968 *un lieu de vie*) for autistic children, some of whom were teenagers. Previously having taken one young boy in charge, he had decided to attempt to find access to these non-speaking children. He settled in South of France in the region of the Cévennes in a small village called Monoblet. He was quite pragmatic—that's why I speak of a magician therapist—he didn't want to 'heal' the children nor did he think he could make them speak, but focused instead on trying to access their desire that could not be verbally expressed. He could do that because he could in the first place just live with them, with them around him, and in this everyday coexistence he didn't 'care' for them in a therapeutic or paternalistic way, but tried to find out how their desire could be approached, even though they didn't seem to possess any language.

Opposed to, or rather, expanding Foucault's society of discipline (1976), Deleuze talks of societies of control as micro forms of control that do not affect the person as an individual (*discipline*) or as part of a mass—a population such as prisoners, soldiers or TB bearers—(biopower) but at the microscopic level of behaviour and feelings. Policy is never elaborated 'once-and-for-all', but always changing, adapting to new situations, adjusting to every single person's sensitivity. When a psychologist in a daycare centre demands that one should not cradle a baby, she tends to require conformity not only in one's way of handling the baby's body, but delineating one's most intimate feelings, gestures and behaviour, creating doubts about one's own understanding and sensitivity. This means that a society of control is not a homogeneous set of commands or norms, but, on the contrary, ever changing, adjustable reticular norms that impose themselves at the most intimate and subjective level.

In a society of control, subjection is based on *loci*, on local circumstances that alter practical sense, perceptive intelligence: a baby's shouting can be interpreted as a non-verbal language that could account for its desire. But how can one get access to it? How could space and time open a path to the expression of its desire? That's where Deligny's experimentation is heuristic and useful. He noticed these autistic children were very much on the move and so he started sketching their movements in the farm and its surroundings. He noticed junctions, turn offs, paths and roads that were used sometimes frequently, sometimes not. So he continued drawing these peregrinations, establishing maps, and doing this very meticulously, he discovered a language, a language of desire materialized by spots where this child would stop, paths that other children would avoid but sometimes nevertheless would use. So all these lines would suddenly make sense for this or that child. He called these lines, '*lignes d'erre*', lines of wandering (from the verb *errer*) and he discovered that these lines of wandering could be linked to moments of intensity for the children, of moments where something 'happened' in their corporal behaviour, in their rhythm in walking, in their postures. He therefore called these lines of wandering the non-verbal language of desire (Deligny, 1975, 1976).

This detour helps me to submit a hypothesis. In a society growing closer and closer to what Deleuze calls a 'society of control' (1990), couldn't Deligny's conceptualization of the lines of wandering be helpful for us to get access to what escapes and leaks out of the strict boundaries that developmental and cognitive psychology tend to demand from staff members when ordering them not to hug or cradle children? If these women find enough energy and subjective strength to resist these injunctions of psychologists whose social status authorizes them to gain benefit from their authority, it enables young children's desire enacted in verbal and non-verbal manifestations to emerge. And so what the research showed is that, empowered by the researcher's attention and interest in supporting their discursive findings, they are in a privileged position to get access to the children's language (verbal or non verbal) of desire. So, I would conclude that this research made it possible to make visible the hidden and unvalued competences of these low trained and low paid women, who nevertheless, on a daily basis, experience, support and enable the liveliness and the happiness of these magic moments when children's desire emerges and they feel, as they say, that 'something happened'. They discover an unknown language that flows between adults and children, something that escapes the usual highways of the normalized paths, the politically audible conformed language. Through their narratives, they themselves discover skills and resources they were unaware of. This access to the children's desire helps us to understand that it may be necessary to consider the language of desire of young children (but our own as so-called adults as well) as a totally foreign or unknown language.

Another narrative can highlight this concluding point.

> Benjamin comes to the crèche early in the morning, Nathalie notices he seems unhappy; he's grumpy and cries a lot. Another staff member Sylvaine tells Nathalie that Benjamin's parents are getting divorced. Benjamin continues crying a lot. Everybody tries to soothe him and the information about his parents' divorce spreads. After lunch, when comes time for the nap, Nathalie takes off Benjamin's shoes and discovers he has a huge blister on the foot because his sock had a hole.

We are constantly caught in logos. To try and start thinking from another standpoint about language means one escapes this regime of normalization, where the verbal and non-verbal, the perceptive and the corporal are taken seriously.

Note

1. Having worked with Félix Guattari from 1965 to his death in 1992, as a member of a collective free-lance research group he created (the Centre d'Etude, de Recherche et de Formation Institutionnelles—CERFI), I was able to meet, exchange and discuss ideas with Michel Foucault and especially Gilles Deleuze with whom Guattari wrote three major books (*Anti-Oedipus, Thousand Plateaus* and *What is Philosophy?*). My work in progress tries to make use of their thoughts, especially my fieldwork and conceptualizations. In his personal work (*Pychanalyse and Transversalité*) and particularly in his work with Deleuze (*Anti-Œdipe, Mille Plateaux*), Guattari theorized early childhood in developing the concept of 'becoming-child' (see my articles on the Reconceptualizing Early Childhood website, 2003 'Becoming-Child in Deleuze and Guattari's work' and 'Narrative on a Becoming-child'. Foucault, it seems to me, never really dealt with Early Childhood issues.

References

Borgnon L. (2005) *A Virtual Child*, unpublished paper.

Canguilhem G. (1985) *Le normal et le pathologique* (Paris, Payot).

Delalande J. (2003) Culture enfantine et règles de vie. Jeux et enjeux de la cour de récréation, *Terrain*, Issue titled: Enfant et apprentissage, 40. March.

Deleuze G. (1990) *Pourparlers* (Paris, Minuit).

Deleuze G. & Guattari F. (1972) *L'Anti-Œdipe* (Paris, Minuit).

Deleuze G. & Guattari F. (1980) *Mille Plateaux* (Paris, Minuit).

Deleuze G. & Guattari F. (1991) *Qu'est ce que la philosophie?* (Paris, Minuit).

Deligny F. (1975) Dérives. Chronique d'une tentative, *Cahiers de l'immuable*/2 (Paris, Recherches).

Deligny F. (1976) Au défaut du langage, *Cahiers de l'Immuable*/3 (Paris, Recherches).

Foucault M. (1976) *Surveiller et punir* (Paris, Gallimard).

Foucault M. (1994) *Dits et Ecrits* (Paris, Gallimard).

Garfinkel H. (1996) Ethnomethodology's Program, *Sociological Psychology Quarterly*, 59:1, pp. 5–21.

Goffman E. (1968) *Asylum* (New York, Doubleday).

Guatteri F. (1972) *Pychanalyse and Transversalité* (Paris, François Maspero).

Hirschfeld L. A. (2002) Why don't Anthropologists like Children?, *American Anthropologist*, 104:2, pp. 611–627 (A French translation was published in 2003 in Enfant et apprentissage, *Terrain*, 40, 21–48, Paris, Editions du Patrimoine.

Mozère L. (1977) *Babillages ... Des crèches aux multiplicités d'enfants* (Paris, Recherches n° 27).

Mozère L. (1992) *Le printemps des crèches. Histoire et développement d'un mouvement* (Paris, L'Harmattan).

Mozère L. (1998) Les métiers de la petite enfance entre compétences féminisnes et savoirs spécialisés, La petite enfance. Pratiques et politiques, *Cahiers du GEDISST*, 22, pp. 105–124.

Mozère L. (2006a) What's the Trouble with Identity?, *Contemporary Issues in Early Childhood*, 7:2, pp. 109–118.

Mozère L. (2006b) Une sociologie de la prime enfance est-elle possible?, in: R. Sirota (ed.), *Questions pour une sociologie de l'enfance* (Rennes, Presses Universitaires de Rennes) pp. 135–146.

6

The Politics of Processes and Products in Education: An early childhood metanarrative crisis?

ANDREW GIBBONS

New Zealand Tertiary College

An Introduction

> Imagine the folly of allowing people to play elaborate games which do nothing whatever to increase consumption. It's madness. Nowadays the Controllers won't approve of any new game unless it can be shown that it requires at least as much apparatus as the most complicated of existing games (Huxley, 1958, p. 35).

Contemporary early childhood educational research devotes much attention to the rationalisation of the environment to meet the needs of the playing child, and increasingly, to the critique of assumptions that construct and govern the nature and purpose of a child's play. Hence the play of the child is not a private activity. The former research trend of rationalisation situates the playing child and facilitating adult in the gaze of the sciences associated with knowing and acting upon play. The latter research trend of critique requires that adults perceive play as a discourse that governs relationships with the self and other—play is here articulated as a narrative.

Two important themes associated with the narrative of the playing child are the dichotomies of 'play is a child's work' and 'process is more important than product'. Both themes are considered in this chapter with an emphasis on the latter. In particular this chapter seeks to further the deconstruction of play through exploring the construction and meaning of processes and products in relation to early childhood education and argues that the distinguishing of process as more important than product reflects a rationalisation of the child and the adult based upon assumptions of appropriate and productive human behaviour. Following Foucault, theories of child's play are revealed as technologies that govern the child, constituting the universal playing child subject, normalising and regulating children and their families.

The chapter provides a continuance of the troubling of themes of childhood and in particular of play, with an emphasis on play as a narrative, that might reveal certain tensions in what it means to say that children play in this way or that, or for this reason or that. Here narrative refers to a story that is told to explain and establish a range of social relationships associated with (in this instance) the concept of play. The playing child is argued to be a grand narrative that has been deployed, by the sciences of childhood, to legitimate the rationalisation of the child's nature and purpose. The purpose of the chapter is to explore a complex play in which the grand narrative, or metanarrative, of the playing child is a site of contestation. Play is then, in this chapter, a troubled narrative. Lyotard's understanding of the crisis of the metanarrative reveals tensions and contradictions that offer spaces to question the theorisation of play, and the outcomes of leaving the question of play to those who claim to have an expert knowledge in things to do with play and childhood—an expert knowledge prophesised in the above passage from Huxley's *Brave New World*.

The intention is not to dispute the value of any shift in emphasis from the products of a child's labour to the processes of a child's labour—from the manufacturing of extrinsically valued things to the experiences of feeling, using and assessing the qualities of media, or of the importance of thinking about and valuing how we do things. Such a shift reflects an intention to encourage a deeply reflective practice. However this does not mean that such a shift should be unproblematised. The very idea that we should look at how and why we do things requires that we deconstruct and critically engage with themes, metaphors, and values—including those associated with the narrative of process. The concern for this chapter is that there is a general absence of critical inquiry into what is meant by the theme of 'process over product.' To play with Huxley's prophesies again, there is a tendency to think of play as a 'Ford-given' process that must be played out in the right order, with the right toys, and in the right spaces.

The Play of Process

During the early 1990s I was introduced to, and challenged by, the assertion that the processes of a child's playful activity are more important than the products of their activity. In particular Brownlee's (1991) influential guidelines for adults in *Magic Places* led to many deep questions about art, learning, and education. The emphasis on process and not product has a history in early education dating back to, for instance, the assumptions of both Rousseau and Froebel regarding the value of the child's play in the natural world (see for instance Cannella, 1997).

The theme of process and not product dominates in early childhood curriculum (Smorti, 1999) and reflects an emphasis on 'the human enterprise associated with and needed for creating products and processes in our everyday life' (Fleer, 1997, p. 23). Here then is an indication that the relationship between product and process (human enterprise) is complex. In addition, Fleer notes, the meaning and application of technology in the early childhood curriculum encompasses 'a way of thinking and doing' (p. 23) and in this sense technology and process become complexly associated with being a child. A child is being a child because she or he is processing.[1]

So how does this apply to play? The answer to this question is delimited in the texts and research articles that reveal process as the play of being a child. For example, Cook and Finlayson (1999, p. 27) argue:

Play is not always to be thought of as frivolous or light-hearted activity for although it can undoubtedly contain these elements within itself, play has a very real and serious functional role in learning processes.

Cartwright (2001, p. 68) identifies process as 'the child's actual work of learning' (p. 68) while product 'means the material result'. In the delimitation of what counts as process, Cartwright posits that children engage in: decision making processes; physical processes; processes of 'freeing one's inner feelings' (ibid.). Here Cartwright is referring to assumptions regarding the intrinsic processes of the child system. These assumptions draw, in particular, upon Piaget's account of the child as an organic cybernetic processor.

Piaget's work in the *Centre for International d'Épistémologie Génétique* in Geneva explains the development of the child in terms of cybernetic processes. For Piaget (1971) cybernetic theory provides an instrumental methodology of revealing the laws of cognition. The cybernetic system simulates observable developments in biological systems and, for Piaget, offers an explanation of how the child's cognitive system develops through a process of self-regulation, or equilibration, in which the system's internal processing of environmental feedback synthesizes existing and new information. The genetic model, according to Piaget, was best represented at the time by the contemporary cyberneticians.

Once an area of knowledge has been reduced to a self-regulatory system or 'structure,' the feeling that one has at last come upon its inner most source of movement is hardly avoidable (Piaget, 1971, p. 14).

The cybernetic question is not wherein lies the source of the change, but rather what has caused the change, and here is developed a leaning towards the vital role of information processing and computation in the transformation of the subject's behaviour. In explaining the intrinsic processes of the child's development Piaget's work (and that of Rousseau and Froebel) has significantly transformed the behaviours of adults. Extrinsically then process theory guides the adult in accepted and appropriate educational practices.

For instance, Cartwright goes on to say that we should not discourage children by giving some products more attention than others. Because the world is uncertain enough, we should not further disenfranchise children by alienating them from their own endeavours. Her intention is to defend a particular valued construction of the young and 'innocent' child—this intention may then be articulated as the process of protecting a universal child self.

Cartwright (pp. 68–69) is concerned with 'true effective rewards' which, she believes, are 'the child's deep satisfaction from the learning/painting process itself: his sense of discovery; his own delight in accomplishment, and not dependent on others' judgement; and his indefinable joy from the integration of muscle, emotion, and mind in the creative work at hand' because children are 'naturally concerned with their own creative activity'. In addition, Cartwright argues that a focus on process leads to more information on each child, and hence a more efficient learning environment. Play as a process then appears as a functional and neutral tool for gathering information that leads to augmented outcomes. In this sense, process theory reflects an assumption that play is a universal process played out by the normally developing child. Furthermore, process theory establishes that the 'effectiveness' of 'true' play is delimited by the 'deep' truths of the nature of the learning and playing child.

This emphasis on the normal child's true play—their unpaid work—constructs a relationship between play, child and society that is not playful. Theorising play as work is a technique of social control and a means of transmitting assumptions and beliefs regarding the nature and purpose of childhood. The player as worker is a subject that can be shaped and modelled according to principles of work—input and output, control and efficiency. These are 'processisms' that provide a self-legitimacy to the claims that play and learning are about process. The child is a resource to be managed efficiently, and hence must be designed and produced to meet the needs of her present, immanent, and imagined work. The playing child is then a realisation of a more efficient means of producing a self-managing subject.

In a pedagogical sense process for a teacher incorporates, according to Cartwright (2001), dealing with the child, the parent and the environment in such a way as to situate the child above any desired product (other than the product of process). The drawing of the parent into this relationship suggests more than a commitment to parent-teacher partnerships, it suggests educators must advise parents they too should not be overvaluing the products and undervaluing the processes. In addition a structural continuity is established between a child's learning and the management of their learning.

In a scholarly environment where a Piagetian structuralism is popularly contested in the interest of protecting the child subject from universalising discourses and limited understandings of development, Piaget's core understanding of the child as an information processor is uncritically transmitted by attention to the process narrative. The information processing subject explores the world in order to compute it, to turn the world into information. Information processing or cybernetic theories of mind and behaviour are influential in claims to understanding and acting upon the child's developing mind and provide a scientific and technological legitimacy to play theory that emphasises process discourse.

This construction of the child subject as information processor is politically exploited. 'Process is more important than product' and 'play is a child's work' are two more slogans to enhance the overarching narratives of the Knowledge Economy and the Information Age. The child as information processor productively and efficiently contributes to a society's information processing expectations. Hence policy and theory transmit and reinforce the idea that early education is simply about process, and discourage evaluation or reflection of the values and beliefs associated with the product of processism.

In Aotearoa/New Zealand the New Zealand Council for Educational Research (NZCER) funded longitudinal project *Competent Children at 5—Families and Early Education* (Wylie, et al., 1996)[2] will arguably have significant implications for child's play as a process of being a competent child. The authors establish that the purpose of this project is to provide the Ministry of Education with evidence of the influence the child's early life experiences will have on the development of later skills and life opportunities. *Competent Children* concludes that indicators of quality in early education are associated with indicators of competence in children. Hence increasing regulation of centres and of educators is claimed to augment the child's competence and, in particular, to encourage 'sophisticated levels of play' (Wylie *et al.*, 1996, p. xii). *Competent Children* articulates a 'shared' understanding and commitment to a universal rationality for early education—a view that attracts little critical attention. The authors produce for the communities of Aotearoa/New Zealand an institutional picture of the healthy playing child that requires no more 'fleshing out' (p. 11)— the subject has been produced, drawn into the public space(s) (Dahlberg *et al.*, 2001) and awaits the will to process in contributing to the performance of the nation.

That children experience a diverse range of services and contexts (processes) appears to be a problem to be solved in terms of providing each child with a regulated service. An intensified Early Childhood Education (ECE) institutionalisation is a solution to the problem of diversity because early regulated play experiences are believed to predispose children to want to be educated—to render them docile—and to offset the negative effects of problematic contexts: to 'temper the influences of family background' (Wylie *et al.*, 1996, p. 2). In other words, to ensure that the product of the process is efficient and exploitable.

Competence vitalises the theme of the working child at play—doing her job well. Wylie *et al.* (1996) argue that competence should not be interpreted in the binary sense of either incompetent or competent because there are no attached mandatory standards of achievements—the authors' categorisation of a range of communication and activity-based competencies are emphasised as goals. However, the language of competence necessitates a technical understanding of the competent child according to a more-or-less measurement of a child's skills/abilities/capacities/dispositions (Nash, 2001).[3] Furthermore, the theme of competence legitimates increased governance of the child, adult, educator, and sector, to ensure the production of a particular kind of competent individual (Luke & Luke, 2001).

This revealing of play as process is a governing of the child subject intended to make the world more ordered and efficient—an instance of what Foucault termed biopolitics:

> By that I meant the endeavor, begun in the eighteenth century, to rationalize the problems presented to governmental practices by the phenomena characteristic of a group of living human beings constituted as a population: health, sanitation, birthrate, longevity, race ... (Foucault, 1994a, p. 73).

Children and their families are governed by the disciplinary mechanisms, observed by Foucault (1991), to emerge during the 18th century as technologies of domination deployed to render docile (temper) a child subject psychologically and physically prepared as consumer and processor of information in the 21st century.

Theories of play normalise and regulate the child's behaviour in the sense of interpreting a child's play as appropriate, inappropriate, social, individual, advanced, or delayed. Experts in child's play construct the means with which we judge the child as good or bad player, and provide expectations of what will happen to the child because of her good and bad play.

In application then, the tendency to valorise the process of play in the present is an attempt to normalise individuals, and groups, as a legitimate playing out of the 'truth' of play and the truth of the contribution of play (Ailwood, 2003). Yet the concern is not the welfare of the player; rather, it is the production of order (as a production of progress) where ordering establishes a matrix of power relationships. The early childhood centre, as an institution of governance in the Foucauldian sense of disciplinary technologies,[4] produces a certain type of processing child. Play theory, as a disciplinary mechanism, provides the principles with which the centre (guided by overarching regulatory bodies) can practice its ordering of the human resources in order to rationalise all resources according to the requirements of technology and progression—the maximisation of exploitation.

The very emergence of widespread early education initiatives and the profession-alisation of the early childhood educator—a social cloning (Baudrillard, 2001) of the organic teaching machine—reflects a process imperative: the notion that children need more organised and regulated preparation for society. Emphasis on processes of knowing and regulating the child's play becomes more important than the individual child's play or play products. Furthermore, the regulation of the play environment transmits the significance of process over product to the child. Hence the playing child is itself a tool with which to colonise cultures and communities where play is deemed to be too product-oriented.

Themes of play as the child's work—the most important process of early education—govern the child based upon assumptions of the importance of play in the experi-ence of individuality, autonomy, freedom, and contribution. However to follow Foucault, it is problematic to suggest that the human self/subject is wholly deter-mined by technologies of domination. Process is not universal. Foucault states:

> Power relations are extremely widespread in human relationships. Now, this means not that political power is everywhere, but that there is in human relationships a whole range of power relations that may come into play among individuals, within families, in pedagogical relationships, political life, and so on (Foucault, 1994b, p. 283).

Problematisation of the power relations that govern the child subject's play has emerged as a relatively recent interest in the philosophy of early education. The work of Foucault, Derrida, Lyotard, Deleuze and Guattari, in particular, has been taken up to explore the ways in which childhood is constructed; how early education reinforces this construction; and how a philosophy of early education might problematise constructions of childhood that obscure the different experiences of childhood.

Research into the heterogeneous child's experiences in diverse situations reflects the currency of a problematising discourse in the philosophy of early education. For instance, Brown and Freeman (2001) emphasise the importance of distinguish-ing between what they understand as the modernist attention to the developmental contribution of play; and the postmodernist attention to the value of play in itself—postmodernists 'value the contribution satisfying play makes to children's day-to-day experiences. They focus on the processes and motives of play and appreciate its role in children's present rather than focusing on its contribution to the future' (p. 261).

This conception of the postmodern position arguably reveals that while the meaning and purpose of education is increasingly problematised from within the ECE sector, the themes of play and process remain privileged—troubling the construction of childhood seems more tenable than troubling the construction of play and process. Brown and Freeman's argument might then be expressed as a reinforcement of the values of the truth of play; and of the child as a playing machine; an expression of childhood as processes to know.

Herein lies the source of a tension associated with understanding and valuing play as an important process, and not product, of being a child. While the purpose and value of play does not remain fixed or unitary between and within the societies often homogenously characterised as Western (Sutton-Smith, 1997; Roberts, 1996), what is perhaps characteristic of the history of Western early education is the tendency to deploy what Lyotard (1999) termed grand narratives to explain a universal nature and purpose of the young child's play. In Aotearoa/New Zealand the grand narrative of play has shifted from the symbol and sanctity of the innocent child (Lindstrom, 1997) who requires protecting and nurturing, to the role of information processing skills that require drawing out and augmenting in order to produce a 'shared' competent product (Wylie *et al.*, 1996) required to participate in a progressive society. Process is then a product of education—hence the argument in this chapter that the articulation of process as more important than product is an indicator of a metanarrative crisis.

Crisis, What Crisis?

This final section of the chapter contends that there is a crisis associated with the dichotomy of process over product. The term 'crisis' draws upon an understanding of Lyotard's *The Postmodern Condition* (1999, originally published in 1979), in which Lyotard questions what counts as knowledge, and the shifting status of certain forms of scientific knowledge associated with modernity. In a sense, Lyotard articulated that 'things', in a postmodern paradigm, would stop making sense; assumptions would be challenged and would not hold up.

> Lyotard places these transformations within the context of the crisis of narratives, especially those Enlightenment metanarratives concerning meaning, truth, and emancipation which have been used to legitimate both the rules of knowledge of the sciences and the foundations of modern institutions (Peters, 2005, pp. 43–44).

During the 20th century technologies of knowledge production and information processing have contributed to a crisis of legitimation (Lyotard, 1999). Previous hierarchies of delimiting, for instance, the nature and purpose of education and childhood, are undermined by the changing contexts in which knowledge is produced and transmitted—made possible, Lyotard notes, by cybernetic theory and microelectronics.

For Lyotard's thesis to fit within the context of this chapter, knowledge of the playing child as an information processor will have contributed to a crisis in certain previously influential understandings of what counts as childhood and what counts as the education of the child. Previous values and beliefs regarding childhood, and how to act upon the child, legitimated in a range of scientific narratives that delimit the innocent play of the child are increasingly problematic to maintain and transmit as founding truths of the child subject in a postmodern world. Postmodernity is then, in one sense, a manifestation of crises of modernity, the playing out of tensions and contradictions that are in some way products of modern metanarratives—in particular the narrative of the innocent and impressionable child. Attempts, in other words, to explain the fundamental nature and purpose of child's play have led to a crisis in understanding what it means to be a child (or an adult), and to play (or to work).

More than this, the translation and transformation of childhood through competence-oriented process discourse, discourse associated with cybernetic theory and hence complicit in the crisis of legitimation, is consistent with the contemporary metanarratives of performativity. Performativity, Lyotard (1999) suggests, is a legitimating discourse that articulates a role for the Modern institutions in a postmodern state of crisis. In the instance of the playing child, the role of institutional education is to ensure the child plays productively. Performativity pervades the play of the child by way of the theory of process. Caring has become educating. And educating is about, in contemporary discourse, ensuring efficient processes that result in the child's increased competence in continuing, as an adult, to contribute to the goals of a society Lyotard revealed as performative-centred. The very purpose of process discourse may have been to send the metanarrative child of the Enlightenment into a tailspin. However, process discourse, consistent with the themes of information age and knowledge economy, makes itself comfortable in the empty metanarrative nest.

The delimitation of a theory of process over product is a way of thinking about education. To follow Lyotard, the challenge for educators is to avoid settling in to a new dominating discourse regarding the purpose of early childhood education. Any discourse is based upon, Hultqvist (2001) notes, what is assumed about childhood. The concept of the process of childhood provides a normalised space in which a child is to be a child; and childhood is a technology that clears the space(s) in which the child is observed, measured and calculated, acted upon and exploited as evidence of the legitimacy of one way of thinking about children and childhood. Hultqvist suggests that contemporary early education discourse constructs the child as a subject that accepts the necessity to work on the self in order to become some thing—however the some thing is less important than the process of working on the self, and perhaps, the product is the self that works upon the self, the equilibrating child computer that is deployed by new media industries to will parents into participating in the consumption of information processing technologies (reinforcing a sense, for parents, that their child is the computer expert).

In the distinction between process and product is a challenge that is perhaps not the intention of the process discoursers. The problem is identified by Katz who, arguably in response to the growing critique of developmentalism and its orientation towards product, wondered how one could govern one's process as a teacher without some baseline object or product (Meade, 1999). Meade (p. 3) problematises this tension, revealing that process discourse situates the teacher's interests and influences as 'counter-productive' to learning because they get in the way of child's productive processing. Arguably, there is no distinct oppositional relationship between process and product in developmental literature. Piagetian cognitive psychology drew out the structuralist relationship between process and product. The child as a human cognitive information processor, transmitting and receiving and equilibrating, establishes that the only universal continuity is that of process.

The process over product slogan is intended to support the value of the child's play for its own sake, and a belief in the importance of the natural playing child; however, when play is a child's work the very meanings of process and product have become problematic. In a sense, the act of disclosing process as the most important purpose of education engenders process as product. That process has become product is indicative of an emphasis on a revealing of real and transferable value to a human practice when disconnected from a product. Processism is an exploitation of the child as a valued resource that links with wider imperatives, values and beliefs, oriented towards the notion of the autonomous and productive individual child.

The importance of play as a process and the importance of the process of 'play with' arguably marginalises the contexts within which play theory is lived out by individuals or groups in the interests of ensuring certain outcomes articulated as nationally, or globally, 'shared' (Wylie *et al.*, 1996)—predominantly a child characterised as a competent actor in an 'information society' or 'knowledge economy', willing to accept her or his role as an investment who must contribute to the paradigm of information processing (Sutton-Smith, 1997). This investment is increasingly brokered by the trained early childhood educator.

A Role for the Educator

As Duncan (2004) has noted, dominant discourses often have very divergent and contradictory outcomes for those who work in the sector. The emphasis on process results in an emphasis on product—we have to keep ensuring we are process-oriented, where 'process-oriented' is somewhat uncritically defined and transmitted. The process can be numbing for the teacher as a product of 'transparency' and 'accountability'. In any instance where the discourse starts to reverberate as a numbing dogma there is a need to get involved in some messy play (which is a valued process-oriented activity).

Process often means, for an early childhood educator, an emphasis on managing each child, and the centre, to ensure standards associated with quality are visible and measurable (Novinger & O'Brien, 2003). The creative process of being an educator that supports the creative process of being a child is suffocated under the weight of process responsibility.

However to suggest that process is not important, or meaningful, would be problematic. The concern is how themes associated with early education are articulated as important: why they are important, and in what ways individuals and groups are required (or allowed) to engage with and act out their importance. For instance the theme of process, this chapter argues, continues to govern what can be said about the young child's play—any value associated with freeing the child to be active and independent (however those terms might be defined) must be articulated as a process value. The legitimacy of planning and evaluating is established by the presence of discourse that reflects the components of process theory outlined, for instance, in Cartwright's guidelines for art in the early childhood curriculum, or by *Competent Children*'s expectations regarding quality early childhood education provision. The observable (and measurable) presence of a curriculum in which these components are employed becomes the indicator that a centre is providing its community and society with the right sort of educational experiences for the child.

In other words, teachers and children are not free to play with their art resources as a valued process of early education; they *must* behave in such ways in order to satisfy political expectations. However the concern in this chapter is not that teaching should revert to a product-oriented process. Rather, themes such as 'process over product' require critical engagement in order to be responsive to micro-practices, to local experiences, and to the idea of difference (Dahlberg *et al.*, 2001; Peters, 2005). Troubling, or problematisation, of the question of process is a political process of playing with power relationships and the processes of 'immobilising' (Foucault, 1994b, p. 283) children and educators within dominant narratives of process, and metanarratives of childhood and play.

Conclusion

There is a continuity between questioning the relationship between product and process and questioning of why and how we educate. This chapter provides a relevant focus for thinking about what we are doing (and why) when we are being educators, teachers, carers, and advocates in the early education sector(s). Exploring the relationships that are drawn together around social and cultural concepts of child development and around research and policy that delimits educational practice is a necessary component of ensuring the community is involved in negotiating any so-called shared understanding of education.

This chapter then supports the work of Dahlberg, Hultqvist, and Cannella (in particular) in problematising the colonisation of educational practices within the expectations of a performative-oriented information society. It argues for a more visible and vocal engagement with assumptions of shared goals for education, for what counts as competence, for the purpose of play in the centre, or in the home, and for the opportunity to contribute to processes of delimiting these assumptions ensuring that 'difference' itself is more than a legitimating narrative for policy makers, curriculum planners, and play theorists.

If the reader, like the author, is heartily sick of the word 'process', then perhaps this chapter has in some way motivated a critical thinking about the politics of early childhood education and of the themes that are employed to legitimate early education practices.

Notes

1. The investigation of process and product from a Heideggerian perspective will be taken up in a future paper.
2. Originally *Competent Children and Their Teachers—Learning about Trajectories and Other Schemas* (Meade *et al.*, 1995)
3. This is not to say that preschool children should not be assessed or that they should be compared and contrasted in their behaviours and experiences, nor that older children should be assessed for the value of their preschool experiences. Rather, assessments of competence require more widespread critical participation if they are to be socially and culturally agreed upon, as Wylie *et al.* (1996) assert in their government-funded research.
4. This is not to suggest that child subject production is the sole purpose of early education. The provision of early education is also a means of providing an opportunity for women to work, and as May (2003) notes, the structured provision of ECE should not be regarded as simply the product of changing views regarding the importance of early education.

References

Ailwood, J. (2003) Governing Early Childhood Education Through Play, *Contemporary Issues in Early Childhood*, 4:3, pp. 286–299.

Baudrillard, J. (2001) *Impossible Exchange*, C. Turner, trans. (London, Verso).

Brown, M. & Freeman, N. (2001) 'We Don't Play That Way at Preschool': The moral and ethical dimensions of controlling children's play, in: S. Reifel, & M. H. Brown (eds), *Advances in Early Education and Day Care Volume II—Early Education and Care, and Reconceptualizing Play* (Oxford, Elsevier Science) pp. 259–274.

Brownlee, P. (1991) *Magic Places* (Auckland, New Zealand Playcentre Federation).

Cannella, G. S. (1997) *Deconstructing Early Childhood Education: Social justice and revolution* (New York, Peter Lang).

Cartwright, S. (2001) Why Promote Process Over Product?, *Child Care Information Exchange*, March, pp. 68–69.

Cook, D. & Finlayson, H. (1999) *Interactive Children, Communicative Teaching: ICT and classroom teaching* (Buckingham, Open University Press).

Dahlberg, G., Moss, P. & Pence, A. (2001). *Beyond Quality in Early Childhood Education and Care: Postmodern perspectives* (London, RoutledgeFalmer).

Duncan, J. (2004) Misplacing the Teacher? New Zealand early childhood teachers and early childhood education policy reforms, 1984–96, *Contemporary Issues in Early Childhood*, 5:2, pp. 160–177.

Fleer, M. (1997) The Technical Language Children Use at Home, *Early Childhood Folio*, 3, pp. 23–28.

Foucault, M. (1991) *Discipline and Punish*, A. Sheridan, trans. (Harmondsworth, Penguin Books).

Foucault, M. (1994a) The Birth of Biopolitics, R. Hurley, trans., in: P. Rabinow (ed.), *Ethics, Truth, Subjectivity* (London, Penguin Books) pp. 73–79.

Foucault, M. (1994b) The Ethics of the Concern of the Self as a Practice of Freedom, P. Aranov, & D. McGrawth, trans., in: P. Rabinow (ed.), *Ethics, Truth, Subjectivity* (London, Penguin Books) pp. 73–79.

Hultqvist, K. (2001) Bringing the Gods and the Angels Back? A modern pedagogical saga about excess in moderation, in: K. Hultqvist & G. Dahlberg (eds), *Governing the Child in the New Millennium* (New York, RoutledgeFalmer) pp. 143–171.

Huxley, A. (1958) *Brave New World* (Harmondsworth, Penguin Books).

Lindstrom, L. (1997) Integration, Creativity, or Communication? Paradigm shifts and continuity in Swedish arts education, *Art Education Policy Review*, 99:1, pp. 17–22.

Luke, A. & Luke, C. (2001) Adolescence Lost/Childhood Regained: On early intervention and the emergence of the techno-subject, *Journal of Early Childhood Literacy*, 1:1, pp. 91–120.

Lyotard, J-F. (1999) *The Postmodern Condition: A report on knowledge*, G. Bennington, & B. Massumi, trans. (Minneapolis, University of Minnesota Press).

May, H. (2003) *Concerning Women, Considering Children—Battles of the Childcare Association, 1963–2003* (Wellington, Te Tari Puna Ora o Aotearoa/New Zealand Childcare Association).

Meade, A. (1999) If You Say it Three Times, is it True? Critical use of research in early childhood education, *Third Warwick International Early Years Conference*, 12–16 April.

Meade, A., Cubey, P., Hendricks, A. & Wylie, C. (1995) *Competent Children and Their Teachers— Learning about Trajectories and Other Schemas* (Wellington, New Zealand Council for Educational Research).

Nash, R. (2001) Competent Children: A critical appreciation, *New Zealand Journal of Educational Studies*, 36:1, pp. 115–120.

Novinger, S. & O'Brien, L. (2003) Beyond 'Boring, Meaningless Shit' in the Academy: Early childhood teacher educators under the regulatory gaze, *Contemporary Issues in Early Childhood*, 4:1, pp. 3–31.

Peters, M. (2005) Lyotard, Marxism and Education: The problem of knowledge capitalism, in: J. Marshall (ed.), *Poststrucuralism, Philosophy, Pedagogy* (Dordrecht, Kluwer Academic Publishers) pp. 43–56.

Piaget, J. (1971). *Structuralism*, C. Maschler, trans. (London, Routledge & Kegan Paul).

Roberts, P. (1996) Defending Freirean Intervention, *Educational Theory*, 46:3, pp. 335–352.

Smorti, S. (1999) Technology in Early Childhood, *Early Education*, 19, Autumn, pp. 5–9.

Sutton-Smith, B. (1997) *The Ambiguity of Play* (Cambridge, MA, Harvard University Press).

Wylie, C., Thompson, J. & Hendricks, A. K. (1996) *Competent Children at 5—Families and Early Education* (Wellington, New Zealand Council for Educational Research).

7

(Re)Positioning the Child in the Policy/Politics of Early Childhood

CHRISTINE WOODROW & FRANCES PRESS
University of Western Sydney; Charles Sturt University

Introduction

Typically a number of 'discourses' about childhood, the nature of children and how children should be treated, circulate at any given time. These discourses are both underpinned by beliefs and assumptions about the experience and purpose of childhood, and inform the social and economic policies that shape daily practices. Historical analysis reveals the fluid nature of these constructions and the ways in which particular 'ideas' of childhood have marked epochs and eras. Constructions of 'the child' and childhood and the discourses that surround and produce them are often contradictory and likely to compete for dominance in policy and practice. As academics, early childhood teacher educators and policy activists, our particular interest is in identifying the contemporary views of childhood embedded in the daily practices and policy frameworks of the field of early childhood education and care. We are concerned with how these views shape the public and professional discourse about institutions of early childhood such as those that we have come to know as childcare, preschool, early intervention and school; how these are organised and resourced; and in the final analysis what this might mean for the daily experience of children.

As the notion of childhood as a socially constructed phenomenon has established itself over the past decade, a literature has emerged that explains and interrogates dominant images and understandings (Holland, 1992; 2004) their consequent meanings in social practice (James & Prout, 1990; James, Jenks & Prout, 1999) and their implications for the field of early childhood (Dahlberg, Moss & Pence 1999; Woodrow, 1999; Woodrow & Brennan, 2001). We have come to understand some of the ways economic and social trends and flows significantly affect the way early childhood is thought about and how these influence policy and practice (Press & Woodrow, 2005). Our recent work in this area has led us to identify an emerging construction, based on the notion of childhood as a vehicle for and site of consumption, infiltrating policy and practice in early childhood education and care. This construction has the potential to normalise policies, practices and pedagogies derived from a commercialised view of childhood (childhood as a commercial practice) and brings with it potential risks to the wellbeing of communities and children.

We believe that the field of early childhood education and care has changed significantly over the last decade and it is time to identify, name and place these changes within a theoretical framework that has as its fundamental aspect an understanding of childhood as a construction. In this article we are seeking to make problematic discourses of childhood and associated policies and practices. However, in doing so we are acutely aware that the relationship between construction and policy in practice is not linear but that each influences the other.

To inform our discussion we first take a historical perspective on dominant and marginalised positionings of childhood in early childhood policy and practice. Our focus then shifts to explore contemporary and emerging policy and practice contexts. Finally we identify and argue a preferred construction, the child as citizen, to consider the policy implications that would flow if this were the view informing policy and politics. What could the institutions of early childhood look like if grounded in a re-envisioned ethic of care and education within a project of robust democracy?

History

Evident in the history of Australian early childhood education are a number of constructions of children and families which, rather than lying static, emerge at particular points in time, become subsumed by new contingencies, and re-emerge. These are woven into the fabric of our early childhood system and for many years have sewn the tapestry of what we do with and for young children and their families.

The formalised care and education of very young children in Australia has its roots in philanthropy and educational reform. For much of the previous century, the establishment and management of kindergartens and childcare centres (day nurseries) was largely a philanthropic concern 'of interest mainly to charitable groups comprised of upper class women and a few progressive educationalists' (Brennan, 1994, p. 1). At least two constructions of children can be discerned in this period of Australia's early childcare history. Philanthropy located the children of the working class and poor as objects of social concern—the vulnerable child, the child at risk of illness, death, neglect and the child who, should he or she survive, faces 'the imminent danger of larrikinism' (a'Beckett, 1939 cited in Brennan, 1994, p. 16). For instance, the Sydney Day Nursery Association emerged at the beginning of the 20th century, at least in part, as a response to a report documenting high infant mortality and had as its charter, 'to preserve family life, to educate mothers in child health and to save babies from death and from becoming state wards' (Barns, undated).

At the same time, a concern with individual and social reform focused the child in the lens of 'becoming'—that is, the child as future school student, adult and citizen. The 'child as becoming' encompassed a dual concern with the future, the future of the individual (development of the individual child) and the future of society (the developing child as a vessel of broader social reform). As such, at the beginning of the 20th century the Hobart based Free Kindergarten Association reported that in their kindergartens children acquired the 'moral, mental and physical training fitting them to take full advantage of the education provided by the state' (Brennan, 1994 p. 21), whilst the Kindergarten Union of South Australia aimed for 'the betterment of humanity' (p. 19). In such respects the purposes of educational reform and philanthropy were intertwined.

Widespread public concern about children's health and mortality was once more the impetus for the subsequent involvement of government in the funding of early childhood services in the late nineteen thirties. The Commonwealth Department of Health allocated funding for the establishment of a demonstration kindergarten in each state capital (the Lady Gowrie Child Centres) 'at which not only will the methods for the care and instruction of young children be tested and demonstrated, but also problems of physical growth, nutrition and development be studied'. (Brennan & O'Donnell, 1986). Whilst the child remained an object of social concern, the child was also an object for research—a subject in the project of becoming, This was exemplified by staff observation and measurement of children's physical development, with every child examined by a nurse each day, stripped, weighed and measured each month. Middle class concern for child wellbeing placed the family under surveillance, subject to scrutiny and requirements for compliance. Parents had to provide detailed information about their child, sign an agreement that they would cooperate with staff in relation to the 'proper guidance of the child' (p. 41) and were the subject of inquiry by staff who sought information from sources such as neighbours to verify parental compliance.

The surveillance of mothers also accompanied the limited government support for childcare introduced during the following war years. Women's use of childcare was closely scrutinised, with women questioned as to where they were going to work, employers asked to report on attendance at work, and in some instances, women losing their entitlements to a childcare place if it was deemed that their employment was not essential war work (Brennan, 1994, pp. 46–47). Here we see the mother-child dyad assuming primacy and open to state supported disruption only in exceptional circumstances. Whilst the Department of Labour and National Service expressed concern about the possible neglect of children in the absence of childcare provision, the need to maintain the ideology of domestic motherhood appears to have been a more powerful influence.

Today, the provision of education and care services for young children, albeit childcare or preschool, appears entrenched although not universal. More than 83% of 4-year-old children participate in some form of early childhood education and care in Australia (AIHW, 2005). Yet its provision is driven by a plethora of policy contingencies, most of which are not grounded in a commitment to children as citizens in the here and now, or to children's agency. The expansion of childcare from the 1970's onward was very much linked to women's workforce participation. Since that time much of the mainstream public discourse about childcare has positioned childcare as an appendage to women and the labour market. Thus the mother-child dyad remains in a re-invented form (the provision of childcare is rarely linked to male workforce participation).

The Present

At the turn of the 21st century we have been witness to an acceleration of privatisation and commercialism in many aspects of everyday life. Australian people are becoming accustomed to dealing with corporate entities for goods and services once provided through community development models, sponsored or funded by the nation state. In relation to the provision of childcare, the micro-economic reform agenda of the nineteen nineties generated a reliance on the private for-profit sector which has given rise to an expanding and hugely profitable corporate sector. The private 'for profit' sector now accounts for over 70% of long day care places and today over one quarter of Australian long day care is provided by the one corporation, ABC Learning Centres Ltd. A recent purchase of an American childcare chain by this company makes ABC Learning the second largest childcare provider in the world.

Alongside this development has been a re-emergence in government policy of a focus on early childhood care and education as an arena for early intervention. Government initiatives and interventions in the area have been driven largely by the weight of research evidence pointing to the effectiveness of interventions in the early years. Whilst not disputing the difference that high quality early education and care can make in children's lives, these interventions are not constructed around notions of children's entitlements (to education, to respectful collective spaces). They are, by and large, targeted interventions designed to alleviate present and future social ills. The child as object of social concern remains, as does the notion of the child as the future, with children's wellbeing measured only in terms of hoped for developmental outcomes.

Giroux (2002) observes how the increasing dominance of market discourses in the context of global neoliberalism has repositioned private interests over public and, as a consequence, recast the citizen as consumer in a process that conflates democracy with the market. In this refashioning of public services, the interests that assume primacy are the narrow interests of shareholders, individual consumers and national economic policies. Social policies move away from social investment to focus on social containment. This is clearly illustrated by the new face of childcare. Government fee subsidies to parent consumers have fostered an ever burgeoning private sector, whilst government funding directed to infrastructure and service delivery is marginal and directed primarily to targeted interventions designed to contain future social ills. Both the market and interventionist approach serve to limit the collective policy imagination about early childhood provision.

Developmentalism is pervasive and evident, not only in the discourse of early intervention, but also in policy discussion concerning preschool and the role of early childhood curricula. In Australia, as in many western nations, various 'crises,' manufactured or otherwise, around issues such as literacy achievements and job skills have emerged in popular and state discourses. One of the undoubted effects has been a gradual incursion of early childhood curriculum frameworks, often linked to school curriculum and vocational outcomes, with an increased emphasis on 'readying' children for the school experience. Similarly, the absence of a national universal preschool sector has generated debate and criticism as once more concern erupts about the best way to 'prepare' children for school. One of the marketing campaigns for preschool education in Australia used the slogan 'early childhood education— preparation for life' a slogan that effectively captures the construction of children as in a state of *becoming* rather than *being*. Implicit in the notion of child as becoming are ideas of the child as 'not yet competent', life as something that occurs later, and a denial of agency to children.

In a similar vein, policy documents such as the draft *National Agenda for Early Childhood* fail to move beyond a concern with the future development of children. Perhaps as a result of valuing children primarily for who they will become rather than who they are, such policy also construes children's participation only as a synonym for 'attendance' rather than as a means of hearing and acting upon children's voices, recognising and facilitating agency.

These images and understandings of children and the early childhood domain, although reinvented, echo previous constructions. Alongside these however, has emerged another world: childcare as big business. What happens to our view of children in an environment where the market competes for a government subsidised parent dollar? The increasing provision of commercialised childcare and growing dominance of publicly listed corporate companies reconstruct childcare as a commodity and moves conceptualisation of the early childhood space away from discourses of 'community' to those of the market place. A new dimension to understanding childhood as a site of consumption thus becomes evident.

Childcare as a Site of Consumption

An established research literature provides insight into the location of contemporary childhood as a vehicle for and site of consumption. However, the primary foci for this kind of analysis have been media and entertainment, the mass marketing of toys and 'educational' products to children, and the marketisation of schooling.

The literature identifies how these sites and trends nourish and sustain the emergence of a commodified children's culture (Kenway & Bullen, 2001; 2005; Buckingham, 2000; Kincheloe, 1997) and alert us to some of the issues associated with the commodification of childhood. These include narrowing the range of 'permissible' identities; development of a self interested, individualistic and homogenised consumer 'kidsculture' that provides little space for exploration and celebration of diversity and difference; and legitimisation of children's autonomy only as an expression of self via consumerism (the promotion of 'pester power'). As Bottery (2005) notes, consumption itself is being recast as a project of cultural self-creation with consumerism 'the best expression of personal freedom' (p. 281).

Our concern is about the ways in which the corporatisation of childcare locates children in policy and political contexts, shapes the discourses of childhood, and produces and limits identities for children. We are concerned for the kinds of citizenship identities available for children and teachers to take up. As communities across the world grapple with increasing racial intolerance, diminishing resources and sustainability concerns, and issues associated with poverty and social disadvantage, the way in which we position children's agency is fundamentally important. As the importance of the early years in building resilient and caring individuals and hence communities, gains wider recognition, we need to investigate the challenges and potentials for those working in early childhood to delimit or revitalize a critical

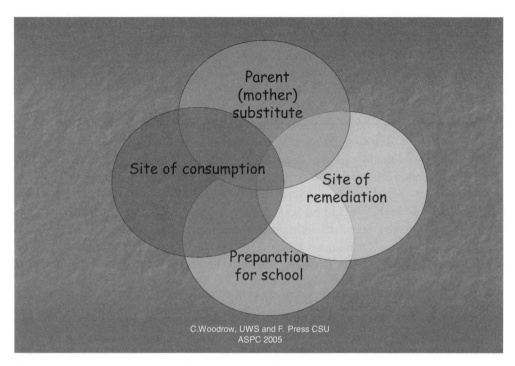

Parent
(mother)
substitute

Site of consumption

Site of
remediation

Preparation
for school

C.Woodrow, UWS and F. Press CSU
ASPC 2005

Figure 1: Competing and changing constructions of childcare

democracy understood, at least partly, as social and political practices through which people can 'produce the conditions of their own agency through dialogue, community participation, resistance and political struggle' (Giroux, 2003).

In both privatised and corporatised provision, children's care and education are repositioned from being a community service to being a commodity in the market place, found and purchased by parents. Such changes in the nature of social transactions have the potential to change the nature of social relations. As Cribb and Ball (2005) observe, 'privatisation does not simply change how we do things, it also changes how we think about what we do, and how we relate to ourselves and significant others'. In respect of the social relations between childcare providers and parents, what might have been previous 'professional-client' or 'partnership' relationships, are reconstituted as provider-consumer relationships. As a result, these relationships become increasingly unidirectional. The consumer role is more passive than active and the consumer has few responsibilities beyond the exercise of initial choice (Bottery, 2005). Bottery warns that values such as trust, respect, good will, sincerity and fairness that have typically underpinned public provision of services are likely to be transformed in supplier-consumer relationships built upon profit motives. Rather than these values being regarded as central to a healthy and flourishing society they become only instrumental to the service of a commercial relationship and the building of greater consumption. The degradation of the status of such values to second order, instrumental status serves to reduce the kind of relationships that are possible between the service provider and the service user/

participant and relieves responsibility for intergenerational concerns and the public interest, concerns that are at the heart of participative democracy.

With regard to the provision of childcare, a provider/consumer analysis is complicated by the fact that it is parents who are the purchasers and the children who experience the product of that consumption. Whilst a traditional purchaser-provider construction of consuming childcare might still be relevant, relationship flows are more complex. It is parents who inevitably exercise their 'market choice' even when such choice may be ephemeral due to tight supply, and naïve or incomplete understandings of quality. Ball and Vincent (2005) observe that 'parental decisions concerning child-care are a complex mixture of practical and moral concerns.'

Bound up in the exercise of choice is the influence of advertising. Corporate providers have large marketing budgets. In the case of ABC Learning in Australia, the promulgation of a standardised, easily recognised 'brand' has become evident. Typically, advertising campaigns promote ideals of happy, carefree homogenised childhoods and freedom from parental guilt. They are targeted to appeal to individual self-interest, and reflect pervasive and persuasive dominant perspectives on the pathway to achieving cultural capital and the good life. Sumsion (2006) invites consideration of how such brand marketing might affect the capacity of the corporate organisation to respond to particular circumstances of diverse communities. Our own research on corporate advertising reveals recurring images of happy, carefree anglo-Australian children, stereotypical depictions of corporatised adults (young, blond, white and female) and texts that appeal to a focus on individual children and their development and learning. These images resonate with Cross' proposition (2002) that advertising positions children as 'valves' of adult desire, as parents seek to purchase for their children an idealised childhood in childcare. Such images are far removed from an alternative vision of the early childhood setting as a social space for the exploration of diversity and difference, the building of critical citizenship and the affirmation and production of multiple and minority identities.

With Children in Their Sights—the Lens of Shareholder Accountability

A feature of corporatisation is shareholder accountability. The primacy of the latter ensures that a company's profits typically take precedence over the social and cultural implications of its products 'This effectively displaces public accountability with public accounting' (Hughes, 2004).

Just as the purchaser-provider relationship limits our vision for the possibilities for the collective interests of children's early education and care environments, shareholder accountability seems to negate the need to raise concerns about the public good. For instance, the Annual Report of ABC Learning proclaims that the corporation aims to keep its staffing costs low (ABC Learning Centres Ltd, 2005), despite the findings of other research that shows more highly qualified staff (therefore more highly paid staff) and higher numbers of staff to children are positively related to better care and education for young children (Rush, 2006). A recent survey of childcare staff found that a fifth of workers in corporate childcare felt concerned about the quality of care and education offered by their centres. This was a markedly higher percentage of concerned staff than found in non-profit centres (4%) and independent private centres (6%). Such findings generate concerns that increasing corporatisation may be having a negative impact on quality (Rush, 2006).

Whilst the chairman of the Australian Consumer and Competition Council, Graeme Samuel, supports government involvement in areas such as education and health, this rationale is not extended to childcare. Childcare services are deemed to benefit from competition in a way that is not considered appropriate for school education, where government support enables a 'high basic level of education' and health services where 'all Australians obtain the best quality of care that they can' (Samuel, 2006a). In relation to childcare, however, the ACCC has ruled that 'Our consideration is, do parents have a choice? Will that choice lead to competition? Competition ... invariably provides for lower costs for parents and higher quality of services' (Samuel, 2006b). There is no evidence to indicate that quality improves with competition. In fact, the drive to lower costs in order to compete in the domain of parent fees is considered to have detrimental impact on childcare quality (Press, 1999). This in itself indicates a disregard for the citizenship rights of young children, as the protection of their interests is subservient to the potential benefits of competition in lowering the costs of care for parents.

In addition, the financial muscle of corporate providers has been used to actively counteract interventions by the state on behalf of the public good (or children's interests). For instance, ABC Learning has recently lost a court case in which it appealed against a $200 fine imposed for breaching a safety regulation of the Children's Services Act in Victoria. The corporation argued that its staff alone were responsible for the breach, rather than it, as the manager of the service. In another Victorian case, the corporation is attempting to stop the childcare licensing body from asking for details and documents concerning alleged breaches of the regulations (Farouque, 2006). Such actions to limit public transparency, open debate and discussion exemplify the potential for the public good to become subsumed to the protection of shareholder interests.

A further concern rests with constraints that the protection of shareholder interests may place upon practice. At the time of writing this article, controversy had broken out over revelations that a group of community based childcare programs, under the auspices of an inner city local council, use books depicting gay and lesbian families. Whilst the mayor of the council involved defended the practices through the council's philosophy of social inclusion, the editorial of one of the popular daily newspapers likened such practices to child abuse (Daily Telegraph, June 5, 2006). Much of the media backlash depicted children as incapable of understanding sexuality issues and argued strongly that the childcare setting was an inappropriate forum for the exploration of such family diversity (ibid.).

Given the sanitized public face of corporate childcare in Australia, it is hard to imagine a corporate entity risking its bottom line by advancing an agenda of social justice and inclusion. Yet social reality is that significant numbers of gay and lesbian families exist in Australia, and many children in these families attend childcare, and experience a life both similar to and different from some other Australian children. A citizenship argument would afford children living in gay and lesbian families the right to have their family structure acknowledged and to participate as fully in community life as their counterparts in heterosexual families. This recent experience invites further consideration of the child's experience of childcare and the construction(s) of childhood that such provision might produce or constrain.

Reimagining Early Childhood Space: Child as Citizen

So far in this article we have drawn attention to some of the limitations placed on children's identity and agency within the dominant trends of childcare policy. We are concerned about the way corporatised provision constructs children as consumers-in-waiting with their care and education increasingly located as a private and individual concern. We have gestured towards the constraints around the kind of identity that emerges from the effects of corporatisation and we have suggested that current trends narrow the possibilities of social reform in the provision of early childhood services. Emerging from our analysis is an understanding of how the child is positioned as the object of social policy, and rarely if ever regarded as a policy actor, a point taken up by the OECD Country Note on Australian Early Childhood Education and Care.

> The ad hoc development of early childhood policy over the years in relation to the needs of parents, the workplace, and the economy, has tended to subsume the interests of children as being synonymous. There are tensions in this, and it is opportune to reflect on current policy priorities from a perspective that places the interests and needs of children to the fore. (OECD, 2001a)

Giroux (2002) (citing Boggs, 2000) argues that as neoliberal policies shrink the public spaces available 'for debating norms, critically engaging ideas, making private issues public, and evaluating judgments' it has become even more urgent to interrogate 'such values as citizen participation, the public good, political obligation, social governance and community'.

The trend to privatised and corporatised childcare provision raises fundamental questions about ethics, citizenship and children's worlds. However, exciting counterflows exist. Underpinned by a discourse of rights, most explicitly expressed through the United Nation Convention on the Rights of the Child (UNCROC), alternative positionings of the child within the framework of citizenship have been strengthened by theoretical resources emerging from the 'new sociology of childhood' movement (James & Prout, 1999), the growing acceptance of socio-cultural theories of learning (Fleer, 2006) and a resistance to neoliberal ideologies that promote individual interests over concerns for collective wellbeing (Bottery, 2005; Giroux, 2002). Opportunities to evoke and support children's citizenship exist at both the local community level, within the practices of childcare provision as well as at the level of the state in relation to policy and research.

Implications for policy and practice that flow from these concerns involve a re-orientation of services, pedagogy and policy to the experiences of childhood from the perspective of children, and an acknowledgment that children have the capacity and the entitlement to have their perspectives both sought and considered. This necessitates a concern itself with the experiences and rights of children in the here and now, not just in relation to 'hoped-for' developmental outcomes. Tucci *et al.* (2004) argue that better outcomes for children may result from 'continuing to re-orient social discourse to the needs, vulnerabilities and competencies of children ...' (p. 15) and the OECD makes the point that countries with high quality comprehensive services for young children 'have recognised the importance of focusing on children as a social group with rights' (OECD, 2001b, p. 127).

In the Australian context, the appointment of 'Commissioners of Children' in several states has brought both symbolic acknowledgement and a research, policy and practice agenda that privileges the perspective of children in social policy and practice. Such offices have maintained a dual focus on (a) protection of the child, and (b) advancement of children's participation in community life and the decisions that affect their experiences of childhood.

The development of the government led *ACT Children's Plan* (2004) provides another example of affording to children the opportunity of participation in decisions about their lives. The development of the plan involved preschool aged children in a consultative process and deployed a communication strategy that enabled their meaningful participation in the consultation. This included drawings and statements about their preferred worlds.

Cohen (2005) states that '... without any real citizenship of their own, children's lives are almost exclusively directed from, and lived within the private sphere.' Yet childcare in all its forms is a public space because children are thrust into a daily realm where of necessity they must be with others, who are not of their family. Because of its location as public space there is room for early childhood to become a site for the enactment of children's citizenship. Such enactment is exemplified by small, vibrant pockets of national and international interest and activism in redefining the institutions of early childhood education and care as sites for the revitalisation of democracy and a re-imagined discourse of the child as citizen. Central to this is a move to reclaim and rebuild democratic principles of participation and equity.

In childcare, decisions about children's lives become matters for negotiation between children, teacher, and parents. Actively seeking and incorporating children's views and perspectives in decision-making (both individual and collective) becomes a means of both illustrating and enacting children's agency. Communities at the level of the childcare institution are positing alternative constructions of the early childhood space and provide an opportunity for practitioners, policy makers and researchers to dare to imagine its transformative potential to reinvigorate community and expose children to 'habits of mind which engender an active and informed citizenship essential to the practice of robust democracy' (Press & Woodrow, 2005).

Drawing on Rose (1999), Moss argues for a broader vision of early childhood as a place for the practice of democracy in which 'minor politics', understood as a creative process emerging from the engagement of people in particular local activities, becomes the vehicle for social engagement and transformation. The re-imagined early childhood environment is one of a physical and discursive space that provides opportunities for many possible projects that, as well as conventionally understood care and education, might include economic and social regeneration of local communities, a place for children's culture and relationships and the practice of ethics (Moss, 2001).

Moss (2006) draws attention to how a pedagogical discourse evident in early childhood provision in the Nordic countries locates holistic concerns with children's worlds. In the Nordic example, the early childhood space is seen as a 'site for human relationships, springing from social interaction' where '... pedagogues recognise the importance of the individual child and her identity' whilst at the same time recognising the importance of collective relationship building. The 'relationship between the individual, the group and the wider society' is acknowledged as 'central to development and wellbeing' (p. 74). Closer to home, the New South Wales Curriculum Framework for early childhood services (DoCS, 2003), has deliberately moved away from a concentration on children's outcomes to focusing pedagogy and practice upon an understanding of the primacy of children's relationships.

Early childhood pedagogues and activists have also been inspired by the early childhood philosophies and practices of Reggio Emilia in Northern Italy. These have provided living examples of the potential of early childhood programs as community institutions where 'adults and children meet and participate in projects of cultural, social, political and economic significance' (Dahlberg, Moss & Pence, 1999, p. 7). At the local level of practice, these programs move beyond the engagement of parents to include whole communities. Children's learning is located in the reality of the community context and children are actively engaged in the negotiation of the curriculum. This contributes to the creation of a set of conditions that facilitates children acting out citizenship and community membership thus going some way toward responding to Giroux' call for 'providing the conditions for forms of critical citizenship and a civic education that provide the knowledge, skills and experiences to produce democratic political agents' (Giroux, 2002, p. 96).

Conclusion

There are many who claim to speak in the best interests of the child and although (or because) diverse positions are often strongly held and defended with great emotion and passion, analysis is not always welcome. Challenging and contesting preferred, dominant and sometimes precious views can be risky and sometimes produce violent reaction (this was no more evident than in the community discussions in Australia about the UN Convention on the Rights of the Child (UNCROC)). However, such debates are essential to developing analysis, and analysis has a revelatory function in uncovering hidden risks and in enabling new possibilities to emerge.

Citizenship for children is highly contested and its expression is often limited to its most elementary features, such as a right to a nationality. The right of younger children in particular to meaningfully participate and negotiate in the public domain is often contested, denied, rendered invisible, silenced. This invisibility and lack of-recognition provides fertile conditions for the entrenching of privatised and corporatised childcare. Children's voices are silenced through reliance upon the parent-provider transaction and remain silenced because habits of democracy are often not seen as relevant to the provision of the service.

Hence, one of the effects of current trends in early childhood provision is the diminishing number of forums for discussions about the expectations, entitlements and mutual responsibilities of citizenship, as nation states divest themselves of direct involvement in the provision of a range of public services. The public space for adults to rehearse debates concerning the risks of consumer culture and identities is limited and there is even less space for children to participate. Consequently, provision for children is relegated further into the private space of the family, located either in the literal realm of domestic space, or as the recipient of parental consumption of privatised service.

We support a profoundly different expression of citizenship to that emerging from the neo-liberal discourse in which citizenship is reduced to the exercise of self-interested consumption. In the project of regenerating a critical democracy, we understand citizenship to be embedded in notions of community and collective responsibility. It includes dimensions of participation, representation, and agency built on values of dignity and respect. Against the dominant Australian trend of corporatised childcare, we advocate for the early childhood institution as a site for the authentic enactment of children's citizenship and a space in which a critical democracy is evident and nurtured.

References

ABC Learning Centres Ltd *Annual Report* 2005.

ACT Children's Plan 2004–14 (Canberra, ACT, Australian Capital Territory Government, Ministry for Children Youth and Family Support).

AIHW (2005) *Australia's Welfare* (Canberra, Australian Institute of Health and Welfare).

Barnes, M. (nd) *A History of the 1st One Hundred Years* (Sydney, SDN Children's Services) Retrieved 3rd November 2006 http://www.sdn.org.au/download/history.pdf

Ball, S. & Vincent, C. (2005) The 'Childcare Champion': New Labour, social justice and the childcare market, *British Educational Research Journal*, 31:5, pp. 557–570.

Bottery, M. (2005) The Individualization of Consumption: A Trojan horse in the destruction of the public sector?, *Educational Management Administration and Leadership*, 33:3, pp. 267–288.

Brennan, D. (1994) *From Philanthropy to Political Action* (Cambridge, Cambridge University Press).

Brennan, D. & O'Donnell, C. (1986) *Caring for Australia's Children: Political and industrial issues in childcare* (Sydney, Allen and Unwin).

Buckingham, D. (2000) *After the Death of Childhood: Growing up in the age of electronic media* (Cambridge, Polity Press).

Cohen, E. (2005) Neither Seen nor Heard: Children's citizenship in contemporary democracies, *Citizenship Studies*, 9:2, pp. 221–240.

Cribb, A. & Ball, S. (2005) Towards an Ethical Audit of the Privatization of Education, *British Journal of Educational Studies*, 53, pp. 115–128.

Cross, G. (2002) Valves of Desire: A historian's perspectives on parents, children and marketing, *Journal of Consumer Research*, 29:3, pp. 441–47.

Dahlberg, G. Moss, P. & Pence, A. (1999) *Beyond Quality in Early Childhood Education and Care: Postmodern perspectives* (London, Falmer Press).

Daily Telegraph, Editorial June 5 2006, p. 3 (Sydney News Limited).

DoCS (2003) *NSW Curriculum Framework for Children's Services: The practice of Relationships* (Sydney, Department of Community Services).

Farouque, F. (2006) What happened? The bewildered parents whose questions went unanswered, *The Age*, 3rd April 2006.

Fleer, M. (2006) A Sociocultural Perspective on Early Childhood Education: Rethinking, reconceptualising and re-inventing, in: M. Fleer, S. Edwards, M. Hammer, A. Kennedy, A. Ridgway, J. Robbins & L. Surman (eds), *Early Childhood Learning Communities: Sociocultural research in practice* (Frenchs Forest, NSW, Pearson Education Australia) pp. 3–14.

Giroux, H. (2002) Educated Hope in the Age of Privatised Visions, *Cultural Studies—Critical Methodologies*, 2:1, pp. 93–112.

Giroux, H. (2003) Youth, Higher Education, and the Crisis of Public Time: Educated hope and the possibility of a democratic future, *Social Identities*, 9:2, pp. 141–163.

Holland, P. (1992) *What is a Child?* (London, Virago).

Holland, P. (2004) *Picturing Childhood* (London, I. B. Tauris and Co.).

Hughes, P. (2004) Promise or threat? Models of the child in media policy, *International Journal of Equity and Innovation in Early Childhood*, 1:2, pp. 43–57.

James, A. Jenks, C. & Prout, A. (1999) *Theorizing Childhood* (Oxford, Polity Press).

James, A. & Prout, A. (eds) (1990) *Constructing and Reconstructing Childhood* (Basingstoke, Falmer Press).

Kenway, J. & Bullen, E. (2001) *Consuming Children: Education- entertainment- advertising* (Buckingham, UK, Open University Press).

Kenway, J. & Bullen, E. (2005) Globalising the Young in the Age of Desire, in: M. Apple, J. Kenway & M. Singh (eds), *Globalizing Education: Policies, pedagogies and politics* (New York, Peter Lang).

Kincheloe, J. (1997) McDonalds' Power and Children: Ronald McDonald (aka Ray Croc) does it all for you, in: S. Steinberg, S. & J. Kincheloe, (eds) *The Corporate Construction of Childhood* (Boulder, CO, Westview Press).

Moss, P. (2001) Beyond Early Childhood Education and Care. Paper presented to OECD conference: *Starting Strong: Early childhood education and care*, Stockholm, June 13–15.

Moss, P. (2006) Farewell to Childcare? *National Institute of Economic Review*, 195.

OECD (2001a) OECD Country Note: *Early Childhood Education and Care Policy in Australia* (Paris, OECD).

Organisation for Economic Co-operation and Development (OECD) (2001b) *Starting Strong: Early childhood education and care* (Paris, OECD).

Press, F. & Woodrow, C. (2005) Commodification, Corporatisation and Children's Spaces, *Australian Journal of Education*, 49:3, pp. 278–297.

Press, F. (1999) The Demise of the Community-owned Long Day Care Centres and the Rise of the Mythical Consumer, *Australian Journal of Early Childhood*, 24:1, pp. 20–24.

Rose, N. (1999) *Powers of Freedom: Reframing political thought* (Cambridge, Cambridge University Press).

Rush, E. (2006) *Childcare Quality in Australia*. Discussion paper No. 84 (Sydney, Australia Institute).

Samuel, G. (2006b) ACCC Approves ABC Learning Takeover of Rival Company, *ABC radio 'AM' interview, May 11.*

Samuel, G. (2006a) Big Ideas, *ABC Radio interview May 28.*

Sumsion, J. (2006) The Corporatisation of Australian Childcare, *Journal of Early Childhood Research*, 4:2, pp. 99–120.

Tucci, J., Goddard, C. & Mitchell, J. (2004) *The Concerns of Australian Parents* (Ringwood, Victoria, Australian Childhood Foundation).

Woodrow, C (1999) Revisiting Images of Childhood in Early Childhood: Reflections and reconsiderations, *Australian Journal of Early Childhood*, 24:4, pp. 7–14.

Woodrow, C. & Brennan, M. (2001) Interrupting Dominant Images: Critical and ethical issues, in: J. A. Jipson & R. T. Johnson (eds), *Resistance and Representation: Rethinking childhood education* (New York, Peter Lang) pp. 23–44.

Woodrow, C. & Press, F. (2005) *Privatization, Corporatisation and Social Policy: What future for children's services?* Paper presented at Australian Social Policy Conference Sydney, November.

Index

ABC Learning in Australia, 91, 94–5
ACT Children's Plan, 97
advanced liberalism, 7, 11
advertising, 94
agonistic pluralism, 4, 12–13
agonistic politics, 12–20
Anderson, Laurie, 49
Aotearoa/New Zealand, 79–80, 82
Apple, M., 10
argumentative discourse, 19
Ariès, 68
Australia, 5, 16–17, 88–99
  child and citizenship, 96–8, 99
  childcare as site of consumption, 92–4, 96
  and early childhood curricula, 91
  expansion of childcare, 90
  gay and lesbian families, 95–6
  government intervention in childcare, 91
  history of construction of childhood, 89–90
  privatised and corporatised childcare, 90–1, 92, 99
  shareholder accountability and childcare, 94–6
Australian Consumer and Competition Council, 95
'autonomous flexible child', 46

Bakhtin, M., 25
Ball, S., 93, 94
Banks, C., 63
behaviourism, 9
Bhabha, H., 9
biopolitics, 80
Bloch, M., 8
Bottery, M., 92, 93
Brown, M., 81–2
Brownlee, P.
  Magic Places, 77
Butler, Judith, 55, 56, 58, 59

Canguilhem, Georges, 69, 70
Cannella, G. S., 85
care/caring
  and gift paradigm, 33–4, 35–6
caregivers
  and gift giving, 28, 29
Cartwright, S., 78–9, 79, 85
Centre for International d'Épistémologie Génétique, 78
Chang, B. G., 54

Cherryholmes, C. H., 11
child
  'autonomous flexible', 46
  and citizenship, 96–8, 99
  development of 'semi utonomous subculture', 70–1
  'essential', 9
  as information processor, 79, 83, 84
  and 'normal' development, 5, 68–9, 70
  (re)positioning of in policy/politics of early childhood, 88–99
  as reproducer of culture and knowledge, 43, 44
'child as becoming', 89, 92
child development *see* development
'child as nature', 43–4
childcare
  competing and changing constructions of, 93
  privatisation and corporatisation of in Australia 90–1, 92, 99
  as site of consumption in, 92–4, 96
childhood, 68
  commodification of, 92
  conceptions of the self in early, 42–51
  discourses about, 88
  (re)positioning the child in policy/politics of early, 88–99
citizenship
  and the child, 96–8, 99
Cixous, Hélène, 36
classrooms, 25
cogito ergo sum, 45
cognition
  and cybernetic theory, 78
cognitive psychology, 5, 84
cognitive theory, 25
Cohen, E., 97
Comenius, 70
common ground, finding, 13–14
common sense, 45
Commonwealth Department of Health, 90
communicative action, Habermasian, 60
comparative education, 20
competence, 80, 85
Competent Children at 5—Families and Early Education project, 79–80, 85
Conley, T., 42
Constas, M. A., 16, 17
constructivist learning theory, 54

consumption
  childcare as site of, 92–4
Contemporary Issues in Early Childhood, 9
continental philosophy, 10
Cook, D., 77–8
cooties (game), 70–1
coup de force, 69, 71
'creations' project, 53
crèches, 69–70, 71–2
Cribb, A., 93
curriculum, 10
cybernetic theory, 78, 79, 82, 83

Dahlberg, Professor Gunilla, 43, 44, 85
Davies, B., 58, 63
daycare centres
  in France, 68, 71–3
  right to place in issue (Finland), 32
decentralisation, 19
deconstruction, 52–64
deconstructive ethic, 62, 64
deconstructive talks, 5, 60–2, 63
Delalande, Julie, 71
Deleuze, Gilles, 5, 16, 42, 44, 45, 47–8, 68, 73, 74
Deligny, Fernand, 73–4
Derrida, Jacques, 16, 25–6, 52, 53, 60, 62
Descartes, René, 45
desire, language of, 5, 72–4
deterritorialization, 42, 43, 50
development, child, 7, 9
  'normal', 68–9, 70
developmental psychology, 3, 5, 9, 44, 45–6, 70
developmentally appropriate practice, 9
difference
  and deconstructive talk, 60–1
discipline, 37
dispositif, 69, 70
documentary methods, 14
documentation, pedagogical, 14, 15, 18–19
dominant discourse, 4, 7–8, 9, 10, 11
drawings, children's, 61
Duncan, J., 84

early intervention, 7, 8
écoles maternelles, 71
economics, 7
educational reform, 89–90
educator, 84–5
efficiency, 9
Elam, D., 52
Elbaz-Luwisch, Freema, 25
empathy, 29, 33
engagement, finding arenas for, 14–16
English language, 7
'essential child', 9
ethic of 'resistance', 52, 64
  deconstructive talks as an, 60–2

ethical particularist stance, 62
'ethical turn', 63–4
ethics, 10, 15, 17
ethics of an encounter, 10, 15, 17
ethics of care/caring, 10, 17, 35–6
ethics of justice
  and gift paradigm, 35–6
evaluation, 15, 18
  agonistic politics of, 19
  and meaning making, 18–19
exchange paradigm, 4, 20, 24–5, 26, 27, 28, 29, 30, 33, 34, 36, 39

fairy tales, 37–8
feminism
  and deconstruction, 52
  and poststructuralism, 52, 56
Fendler, Lynn, 9, 46–7
Finland, 30, 37
  early childhood education and care guidelines, 4, 31–3, 36, 38
Finlayson, H., 77–8
Fleer, M., 77
flexibility, 9
Foucault, Michel, 5, 10, 16, 56, 58–9, 68, 69, 70, 73, 76, 80, 81
foundationalism/foundationalists, 4, 14, 17
France
  daycare centres, 68, 71–3
free creating, 43–4
Free Kindergarten Association, 89
free play, 43
Freeman, N., 81–2
Froebel, Friedrich, 4, 30–1, 38, 70, 77
  Muter und Koselieder, 31

gay/lesbian families, 95–6
gender
  and children's play, 37
  and market 28
geophilosophy, 42
Gesell, Arnold, 44
gift paradigm, 4, 24–39
  and aims and goals, 36–7
  and caring, 33–4, 35–6
  concept of in early childhood education, 27–30
  description, 25–7
  and exchange paradigm, 24–5, 26, 27
  and fairy tales, 37–8
  Finnish guidelines on early childhood education and care, 4, 31–3, 36, 38
  and Froebel's kindergarten, 30–1
  and language, 26–7
  and market, 27
  and metaphor, 25
  and Montessori, 31
  play and toys, 37–8
  promotion of in early childhood education, 36–8

in teachers' stories, 34–5
and turn-taking, 33–4
and 'voice', 25, 36
and women, 25
Giroux, H., 91, 96, 98
globalization, 27
Goffman, Erving, 71
Gorostiaga, J., 20
Guattari, Felix, 5, 42, 68

Habermas, Jürgen, 60
Halpin, D., 12
'hegemonic globalisation', 7
Hirschfeld, Lawrence, 70–1
hitting, 34
Hultqvist, 83, 85
Huxley, Aldous
Brave New World, 76, 77

identity, 43, 49–50
as natural or socially constructed, 43–4
individualism, 33
information processor, child as, 79, 83, 84
institutionalisation of childhood, 18
instrumental rationality, 7, 10
intelligibility
and postmodernism, 16–17
interactive pedagogy, 9

Jansson, Tove, 38
Johnson, Mark, 25

Katz, 83–4
Kihlbom, Ulrik, 62
Kindergarten Union of South Australia, 89–90
kindergartens, 19, 30–1, 70, 89–90
knowledge, 8

lack, 69
Lakoff, George, 25
language, 5, 56, 68–75
of desire, 5, 72–4
and gift paradigm, 26–7
Lather, P., 62, 63
learning stories, 14
life-long learning, 47
linear progress, 7
lines of flight, 50–1, 70
lines of wandering, 5, 74
linguistic turn
and poststructural theory, 54
Lyotard, J-F., 5, 77, 82–3
The Postmodern Condition, 82

MacNaughton, G., 16
map-drawing, 61
market, 27–8
as aberrant communicative mechanism, 26–7

creation of scarcity by, 29
and gender 28
Marx, Karl, 24
Meade, A., 84
meaning-making, 18–19, 54, 60, 64
metanarrative crisis, 5, 76–86
metaphors, 25, 30, 37
modernity/modernists, 7–8, 10–11, 15, 19, 20
Montessori, Maria, 4, 30, 31, 38
Discovery of the Child, 31
Montessori school (Texas), 29
moomins, 38
More, Thomas, 12
Moss, P., 97–8
mothering
and gift paradigm, 25–6, 28
Mouffe, C., 12–13, 14

narrative(s)
notion of, 3–4
play as, 76–7
student teachers', 57–60
National Agenda for Early Childhood, 92
National Curriculum of Early Childhood Education and Care (Finland), 30, 31–2, 36
neoliberalism, 7, 9, 12, 91, 96
'new sociology of childhood' movement, 96
New Zealand, 82
New Zealand Council for Educational Research (NZCER), 79–80
Nietzsche , F., 45, 69
Noddings, N., 35
non-nurturing, 34, 37
Nona, Stella, 42–3, 48, 50
Nordic countries, 98
'normal' development, 5, 68–9, 70
normalization
development of in French daycare centres, 71–3
norms, 69, 70
nursery education, 19

objectivity, 7
Odysseus, 49
OECD, 96, 97
Other, 5, 9, 63–4
other-orientation, 29, 33, 36, 38

paradigmatic divide, 7–21
pathos, 69
Paulston, R., 20
pedagogical documentation, 14, 15, 18–19
pedagogistas, 19
'pedagogy of listening', 15
perfomative subjectivity, 56
performativity, 83
Phenomenology of Spirit, 64
philanthropy, 69, 89, 90
Piaget, Jean, 44, 78, 79

play, 5, 37, 76, 83
  as child's work, 79, 84
  emphasis on process over product of, 77–85
  free, 43
  and gender, 37
  and gift paradigm, 37–8
  as a narrative, 76–7
  and postmodernism, 81–2
  problematisation of power relations governing,
    81–2
  regulation of, 81
pluralism, 4
political engagement, 12
political-analytical paradigm, 8
politics, agonistic, 12–20
Popkewitz, T., 20–1
positivist paradigms, 8, 31
postcolonialism, 8, 9
postfoundationalism/postfoundationalists, 4, 8–9,
    10–11, 12, 14–15, 16–17, 20
postmodern ethics, 10, 17
postmodernism, 8, 10, 16–17, 81–2, 83
poststructuralism, 5, 8, 54, 55
  feminist, 52, 56
power, 57
practice–theory dichotomy, 5, 52–65
process
  emphasis over product in child's play, 77–85
psychiatry, 69
psychoanalysis, 70

quality, 9, 18

recognition, 45
Reconceptualist group conferences, 8
Reggio Emilia, 14, 15–16, 19, 98
Reggio Institute (Stockholm), 16
regulation, 8, 19
representation, 45
response-ability, 9
reterritorializaton, 42, 43, 50
rewards and punishments, 24, 28, 30, 34, 36
Rinaldi, C., 15–16
Rose, Nicolas, 47, 97

St. Pierre, E. A., 16–17, 57
Samuel, Graeme, 95
Sand, Monica, 49–50
Santos, B. de S., 7, 19
Scott, Joan, 58
self-reflection, 64
shareholder accountability
  and childcare, 94–6
social mapping, 20
society of discipline, 73
structure/superstructure distinction, 24

student teachers, 56–7
  and deconstructive talks, 61–2
  as learning subject, 56–7
  narratives, 5, 57–60
  and subjectification, 58–60
subject–object dichotomy, 54
subjectification, 9, 58–60
subjectivity, 56, 58, 63
Sumsion, J., 94
surfing imagery, 5, 42–3, 48, 50
Sweden, 16
  early childhood teacher education programmes,
    53–65
  pre-schools, 44, 52
swinging, 49
Sydney Day Nursery Association, 89

Taguchi, Lenz, 44
teacher education programmes, 5, 53–65
teachers
  and deconstructive talks, 61–2
  and exchange paradigm, 36
  and gift paradigm, 28, 34–5, 36, 38
  new professionalism, 63
  see also student teachers
technical practice, 7, 10
territorializing identities, 42–51
theory–practice dichotomy, 5, 43, 54–6, 64
thinking, 44–5
Tiilikka, A., 33
toys, 37–8
Tucci, J. *et al.*, 97
turn-taking
  and gift paradigm, 33–4

UN Convention on the Rights of the Child, 31,
    96, 98
under erasure, 52, 53, 60
United States
  early childhood work, 8
universability, 7
utopianism, 12

Välimäki, Anna-Leena, 31
Vaughan, G., 25, 26, 36
Vincent, C., 94
'voice'
  and gift paradigm, 25, 36

Walkerdine, V., 59
walking, 43, 44, 48, 50
whole child education, 9, 46–7
women
  Fröebel on, 30
  and gift paradigm, 25
Wylie, C. *et al.*, 80